Music Theory for Singers

Level Four

Second Edition

Sarah Sandvig

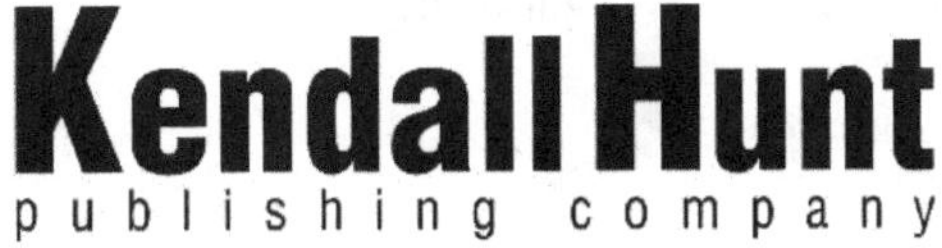

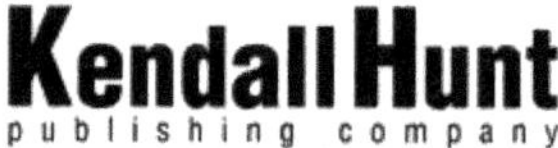

www.kendallhunt.com
Send all inquiries to:
4050 Westmark Drive
Dubuque, IA 52004-1840

ISBN 978-1-5249-1439-4

Published in the United States of America

FOREWORD

In Sarah Sandvig's *Music Theory for Singers*, voice students and their teachers finally have a singer-friendly primer for musicianship and music theory that is directly applicable to voice training. Mrs. Sandvig has capitalized on her experience as a successful private voice teacher to create this comprehensive workbook, which, in clear, concise language, lays out an easy-to-follow lesson plan progressing from basic through advanced skills. *Music Theory for Singers* is equally applicable in a college or high school classroom setting as in the private studio, and voice teachers will especially appreciate the inclusion of international musical terminology, and music history which their students are likely to encounter in vocal repertoire. For teens studying voice for the first time, as well as for life-long adult singers, *Music Theory for Singers* will become a valued adjunct to any level of vocal study.

Juliana Gondek
Metropolitan Opera soloist and
Prize-winning international recording artist
Professor and Chair, Division of Voice Studies
UCLA

I am beginning my first semester as a BFA Musical Theatre Major at The Boston Conservatory at Berklee. I used Sarah's theory books throughout high school from levels 5 through 10, and they have prepared me immensely for this first semester – and beyond. For example, I recently went through a music theory and sight singing placement test: I was so amazed how comfortable I felt with both the written and singing portions. It was everything I had already learned from these theory books – key signatures, scales, rhythm, solfege, and more. In addition, I became so familiar with the fundamentals of music and a piano keyboard (even through utilizing the vocal theory books) I was able to test out of a whole year of beginner piano. All of this creates the possibility for me to move on to higher levels and be more challenged than if I had to start from the basics. Not to mention all of the composers and terms that are necessary knowledge to be successful in professional music classes and settings. It feels good to know that if I am ever unsure about what I am learning in class, my theory books are right there on the bookshelf to help me out.

Sofia Ross
Musical Theatre Major
Boston Conservatory

Thank you to the following people for their help and guidance in writing these books: Mary Beard, Melissa Caldretti, Sally Curry, Sharlae Jenkins, Vanessa Parvin, Connie Venti & my dad, Ken Watson.

Thank you to my husband Darren and sons Aiden & Caleb for their love, support and patience throughout this writing process.

NOTE TO TEACHER:
These books are a supplement to private, group or classroom voice lessons, and though I feel they can stand alone, they are not meant as a replacement for a good teacher who ensures student learning and understanding of music theory, history, and sight-singing. Each book includes reviews of subjects with a review test (with answers) at the end. You may also purchase the Answer Key, which has answers to all pages in each level, 1-10. Composers, terms, IPA and solfege are unique elements of these books that make them especially helpful for singers.

I hope these books are a useful addition to the many tools you already utilize to teach young singers in your studio or classroom.

TABLE OF CONTENTS

MUSIC THEORY FOR SINGERS

LEVEL 4

Review of Concepts in Level 3

Notes, Rhythm & Time Signtaure: Review

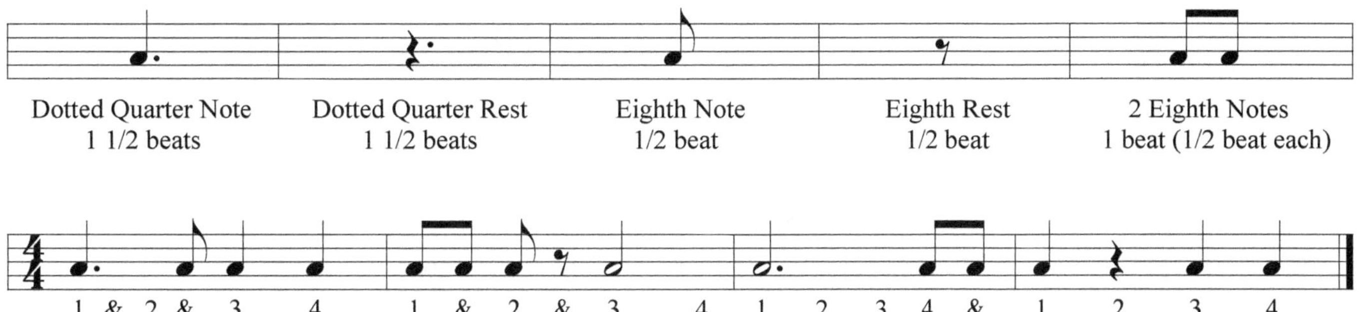

Key Signature & Triad Review

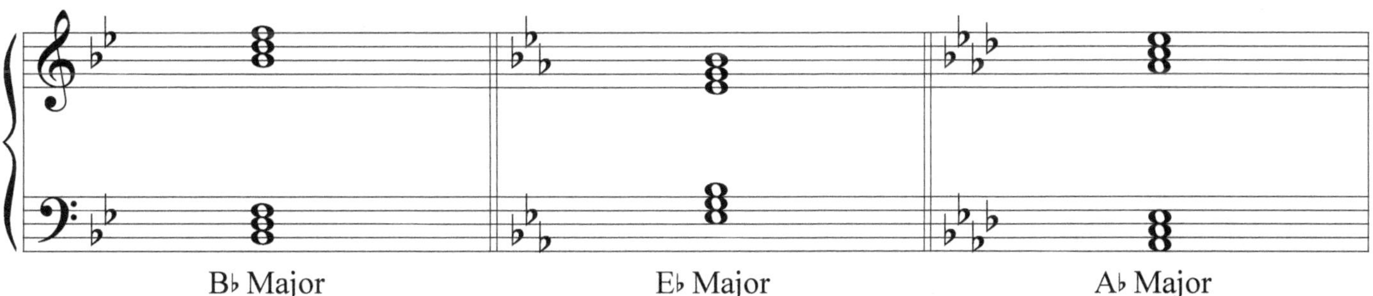

Interval Review

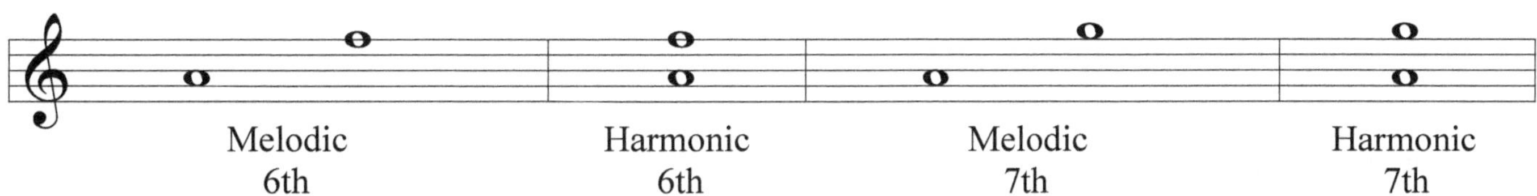

Notes on the Staff Review

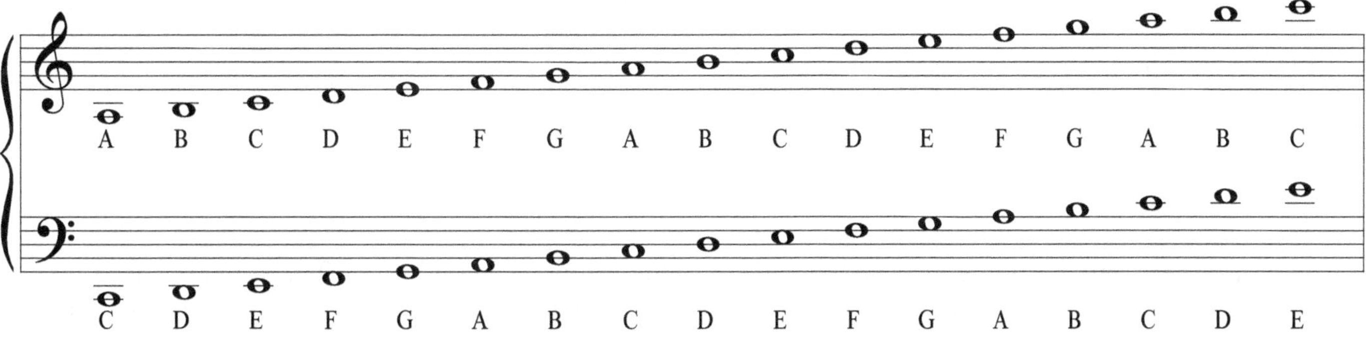

IPA/Diction Review

IPA SYMBOL	SOUND IN ENGLISH WORD	IPA SPELLING OF WORD	TONGUE/LIPS PLACEMENT
i	ski	[ski]	Center of tongue is high Lips relaxed
ɛ	led	[lɛd]	Low tongue Lips relaxed
ɑ	father	[ˈfɑðər]	Low tongue Lips relaxed
o	obey	[oʊˈbeɪ]	Low tongue, tip behind bottom teeth Rounded lips
u	goose	[gus]	Low tongue, tip behind bottom teeth Rounded lips
ɪ	kit	[kit]	High tongue, sides touching top teeth Lips relaxed
e	egg (first vowel sound you hear)	[feɪs]	High tongue, sides touching top teeth Lips relaxed
ə	afraid	[əˈfreɪd]	Mid tongue, tip behind bottom teeth
æ	cat	[kæt]	Mid tongue, tip behind bottom teeth Lips slightly horizontal
ʊ	book	[bʊk]	Low tongue, tip below bottom teeth Lips relaxed
ʌ	strut	[strʌt]	Low tongue, tip behind bottom teeth Lips relaxed
ɔ	forest	[fɔrəst]	Low tongue, tip behind bottom teeth Lips slightly rounded

Sight-Singing Review

Rhythm

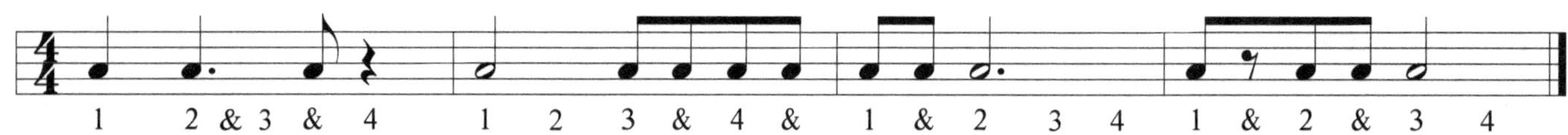

Melodic (with Solfege)*

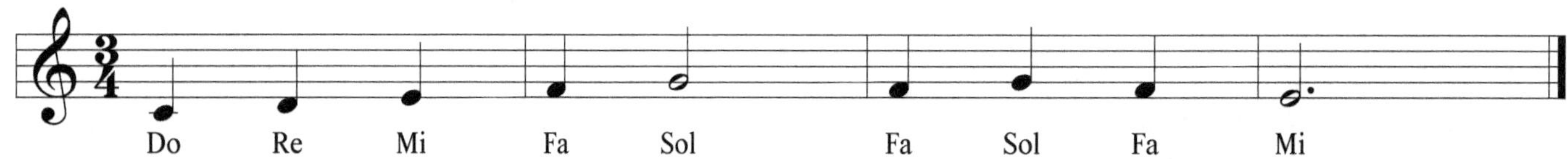

*The Solfege system assigns a syllable to each note of a scale starting with Do. The syllables used for a major scale are: Do Re Mi Fa Sol La Ti Do. Solfege has been in existence for more than 1,000 years!

Lesson 1: Half Steps and Whole Steps

A **Half Step** is the distance between one pitch and the very next pitch, higher or lower. The piano below shows the half steps. Notice the "natural half steps" that occur between 2 white notes: E-F and C-B.

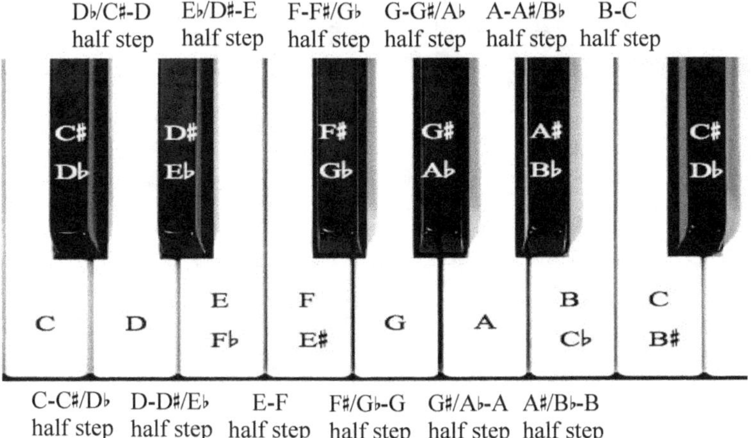

A **Whole Step** is the same as two half steps. In singing, Do-Re is a whole step. For example, in the key of C Major, C-D is Do-Re. There is one pitch, C# or D♭ in between the two notes that make up a whole step. Look at the piano below to see the whole steps.

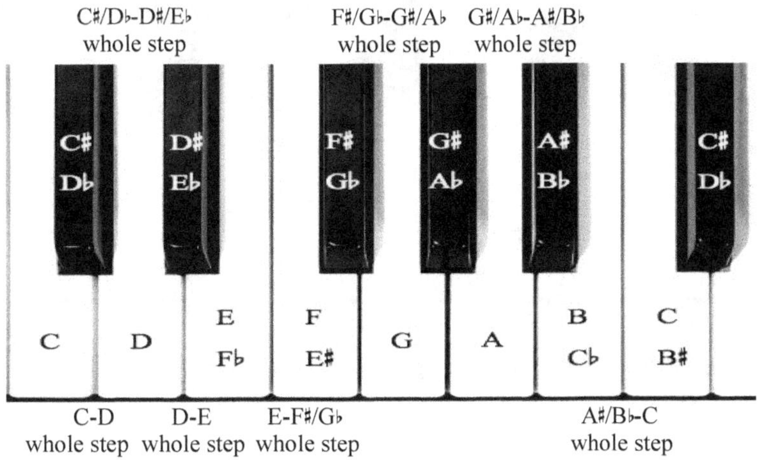

In any Major Scale, the pattern of half steps and whole steps is: W-W-H-W-W-W-H

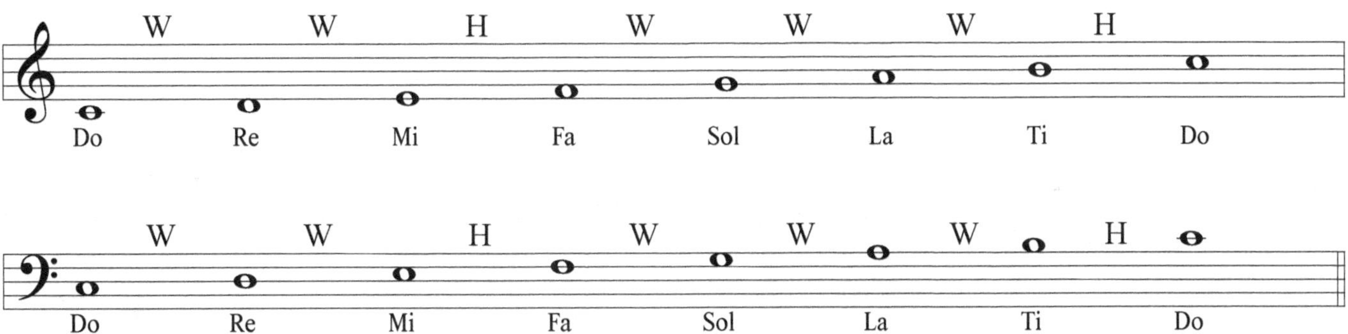

When identifying half steps and whole steps in different key signatures, you must take the sharps and flats into consideration. Look at the examples below, then find the notes on the piano to see the distance between them.

half step — A - B♭
half step — F♯ - G
whole step — A♭ - B♭
whole step — B♭ - C

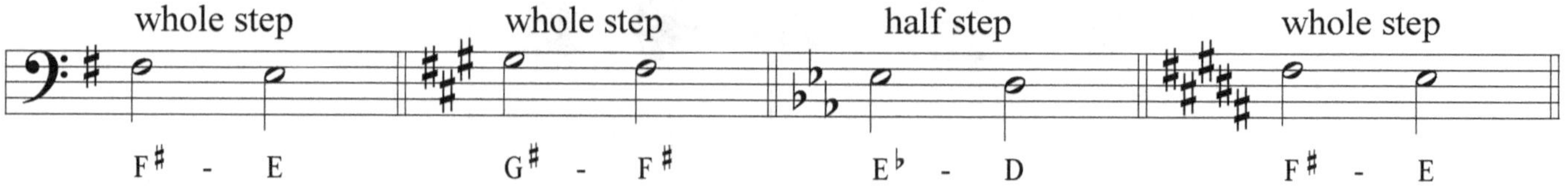

whole step — F♯ - E
whole step — G♯ - F♯
half step — E♭ - D
whole step — F♯ - E

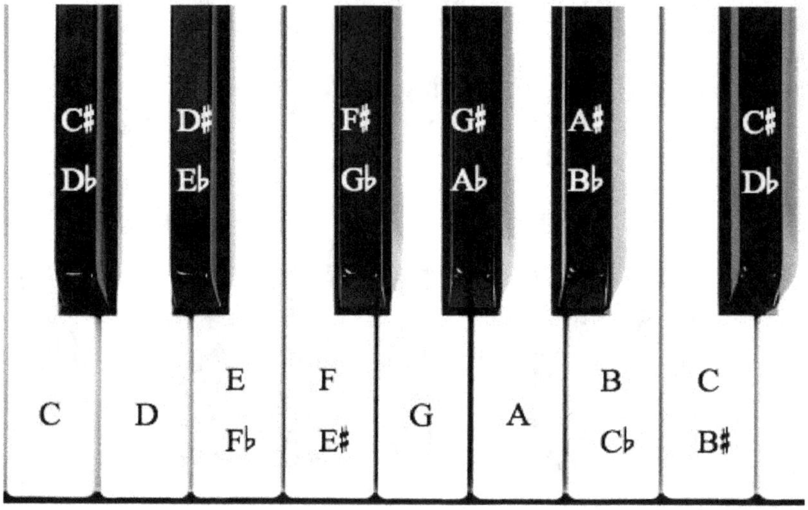

C♯ D♭ | D♯ E♭ | F♯ G♭ | G♯ A♭ | A♯ B♭ | C♯ D♭

C | D | E F♭ | F E♯ | G | A | B C♭ | C B♯

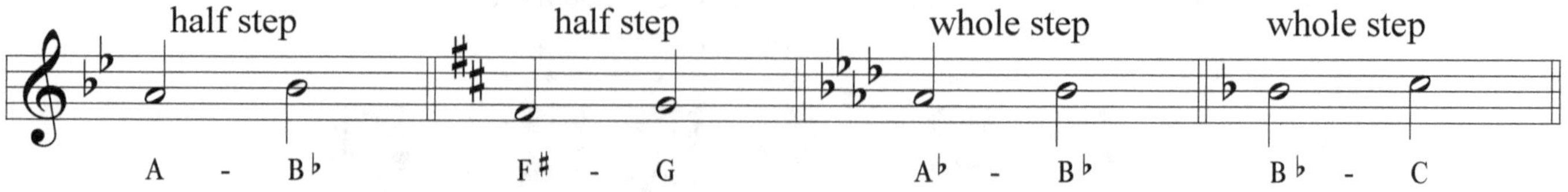

Here are some examples with the accidentals (♯/♭) written in, rather than in the key signature. Find these notes on the piano above to see the distance between them.

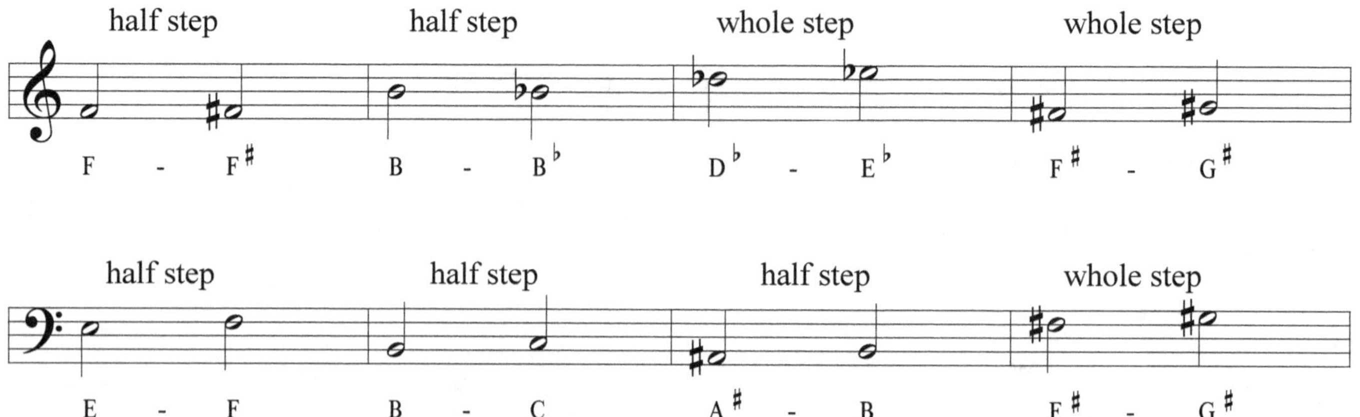

Review: Lesson 1

1. Check the correct answer for the questions below.

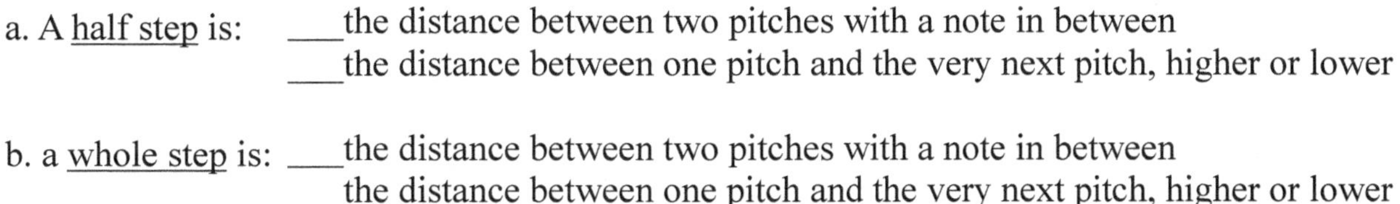

a. A half step is: ___the distance between two pitches with a note in between
___the distance between one pitch and the very next pitch, higher or lower

b. a whole step is: ___the distance between two pitches with a note in between
___the distance between one pitch and the very next pitch, higher or lower

2. Write the notes names under each note, then add an H for half step or W for whole step under each measure. Pay attention to clef changes! The first one is done for you. Refer to the piano at the bottom of the page for help.

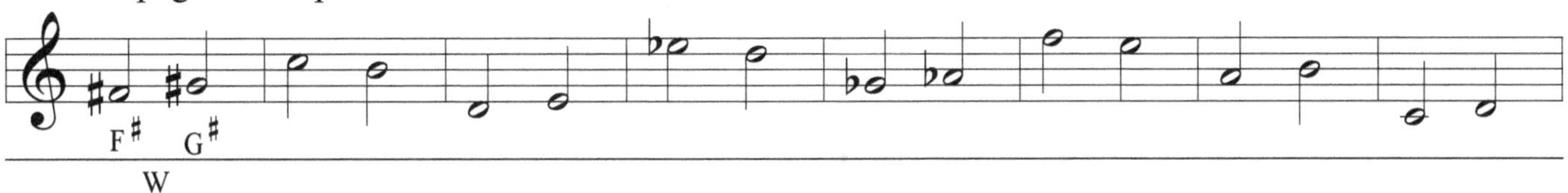

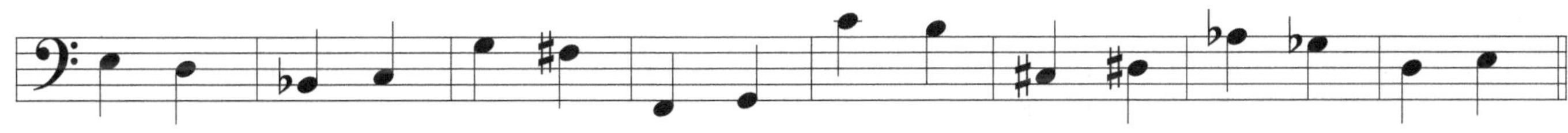

3. Write the notes names under each note, then add an H for half step or W for whole step under each measure. Pay attention to key signature and clef changes! The first one is done for you. Refer to the piano at the bottom of the page for help.

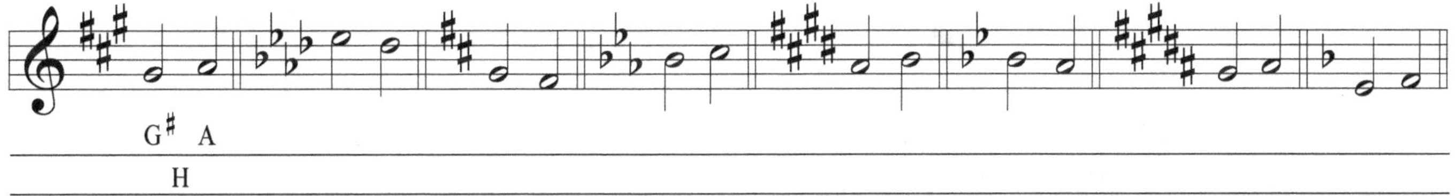

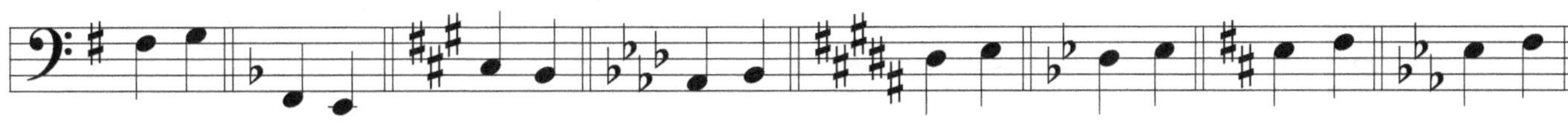

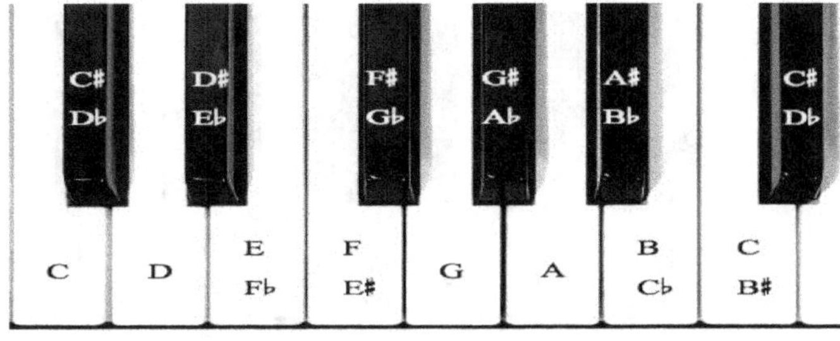

4. Draw the note a <u>half step</u> **<u>higher</u>** then the one given. Use half notes. The first one is done for you.

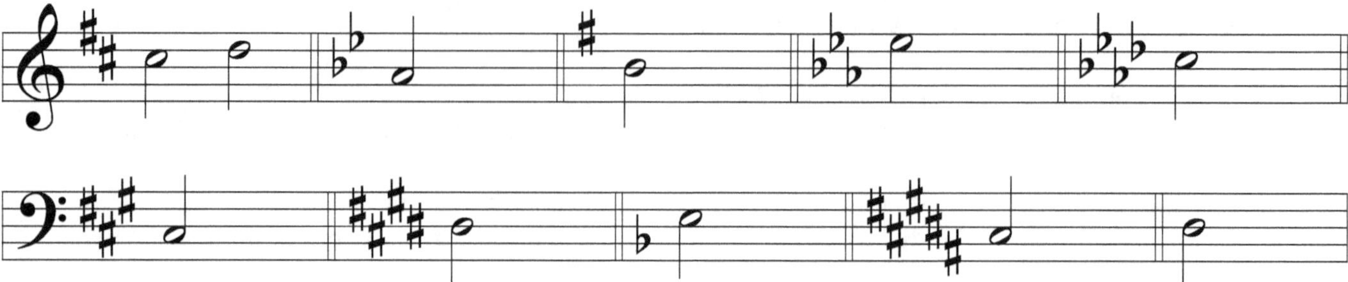

5. Draw the note a <u>whole step</u> **<u>higher</u>** than the one given. Use half notes. The first one is done for you.

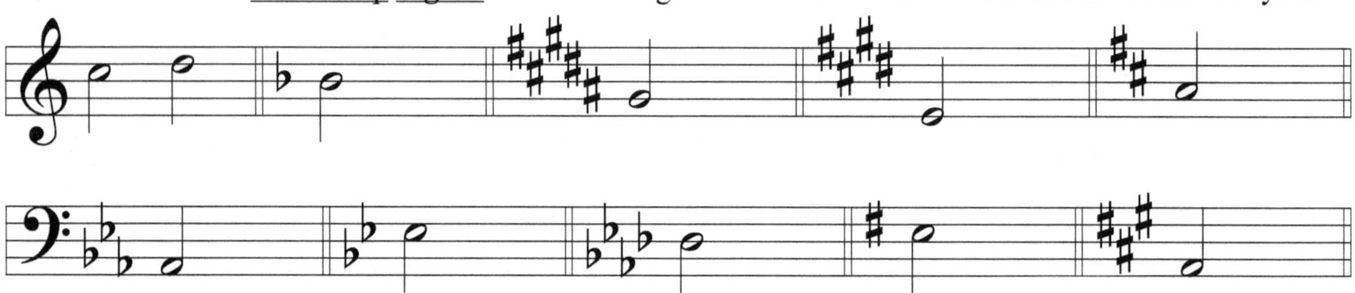

6. Draw the note a <u>half step</u> **lower** than the one given. You may need to add an accidental (♯/♭).
Use quarter notes. The first one is done for you.

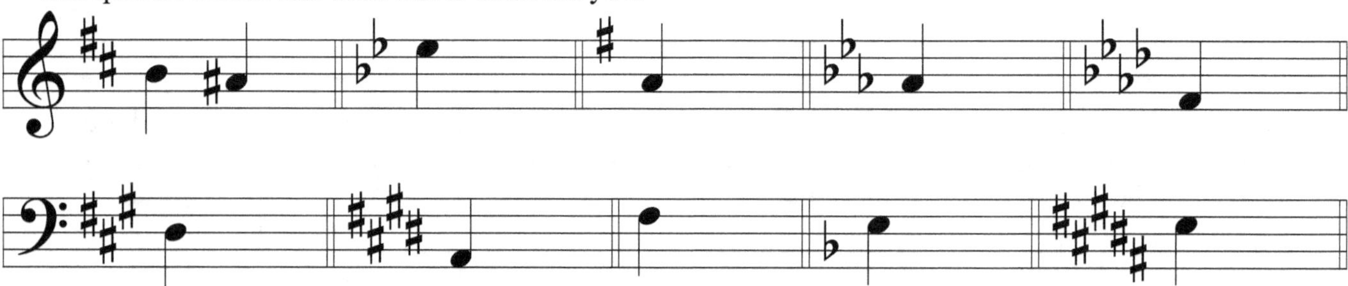

7. Draw the note a <u>whole step</u> **<u>lower</u>** than the one given. You may need to add an accidental.
Use quarter notes. The first one is done for you.

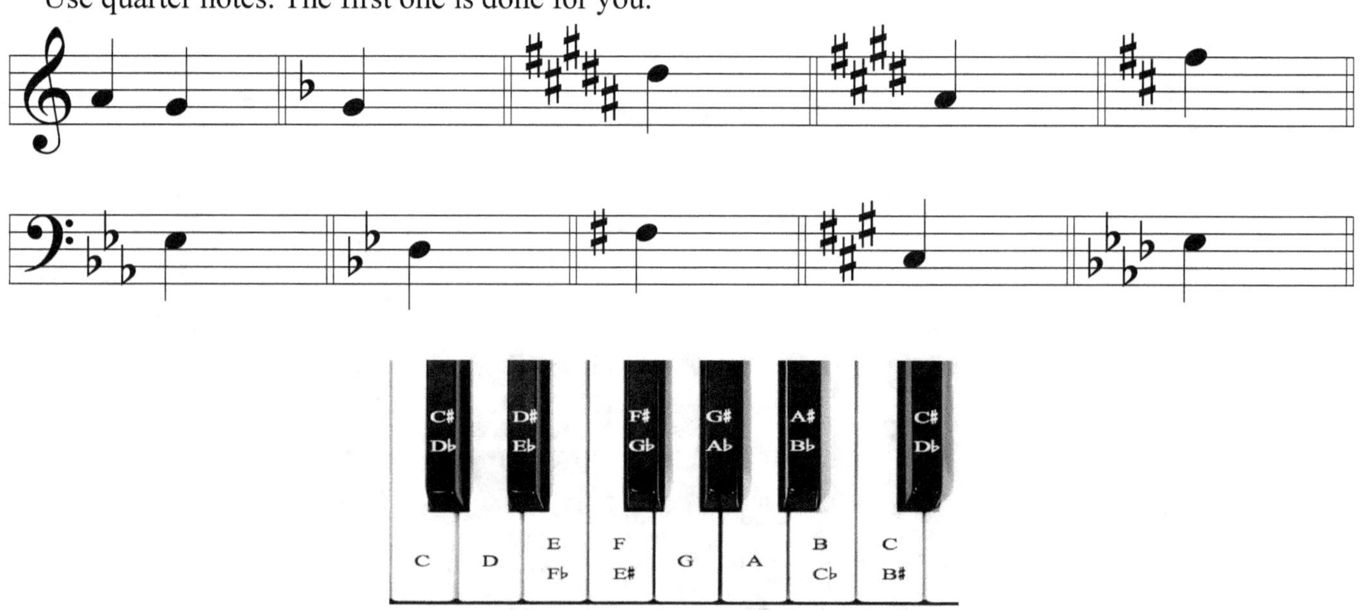

Lesson 2: Note & Rest Values

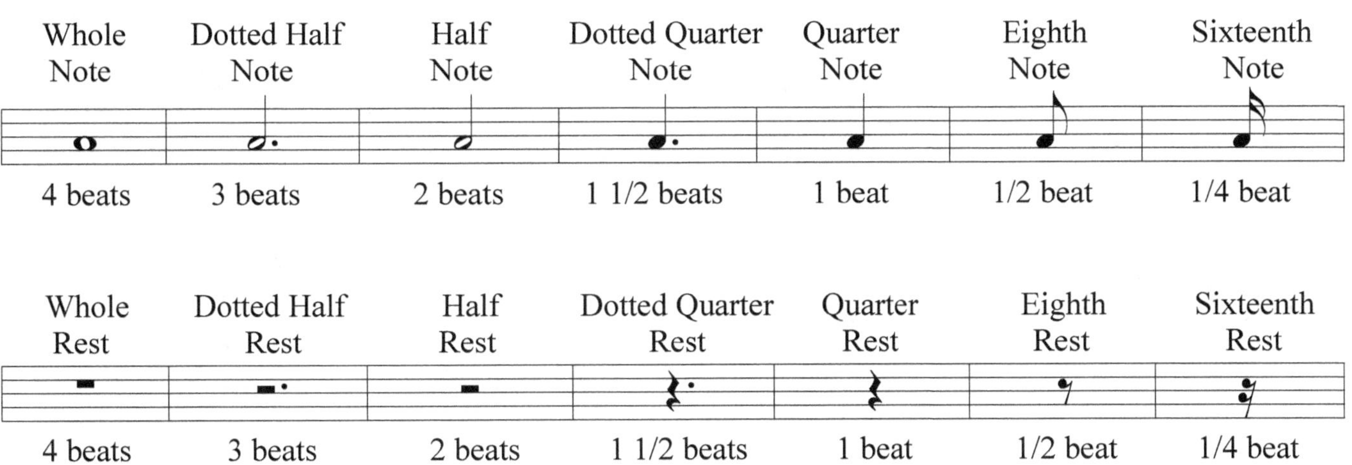

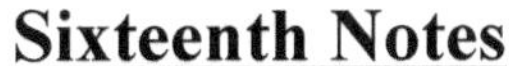

Sixteenth Notes

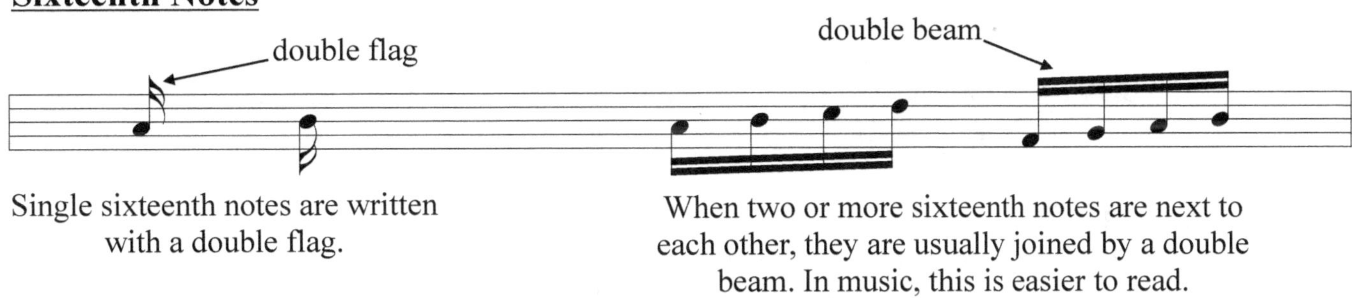

Single sixteenth notes are written with a double flag.

When two or more sixteenth notes are next to each other, they are usually joined by a double beam. In music, this is easier to read.

To help figure out the rhythms, it helps to say something for every note and rest we see. That's why we have 1 & 2 &, etc. Look at the examples below, and sing each measure with the beats underneath. Try to sing the rhythms in the measure while tapping a steady beat.

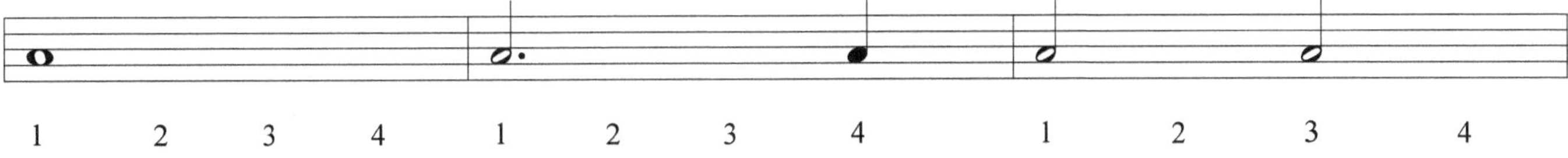

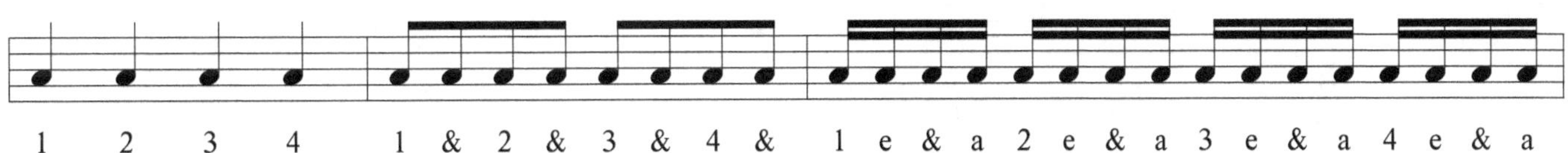

A sixteenth note or rest is worth 1/4 of a beat. In 4/4 time, it takes 4 sixteenth notes to equal one beat. Look at the following rhythmic examples that include sixteenth notes. A

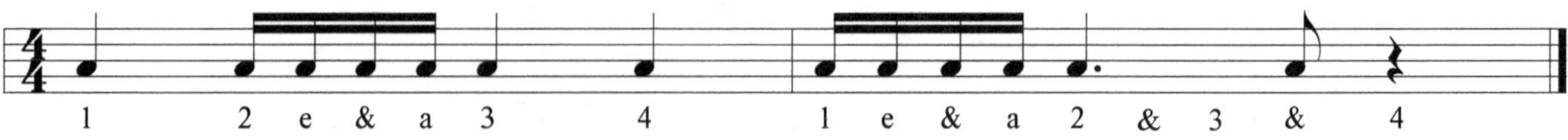

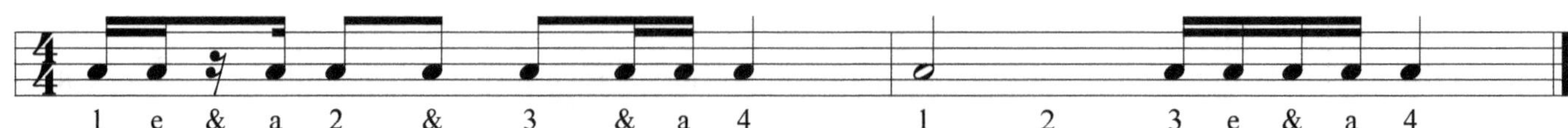

Four sixteenth notes fit into one quarter note. Two sixteenth notes fit into an eighth note.

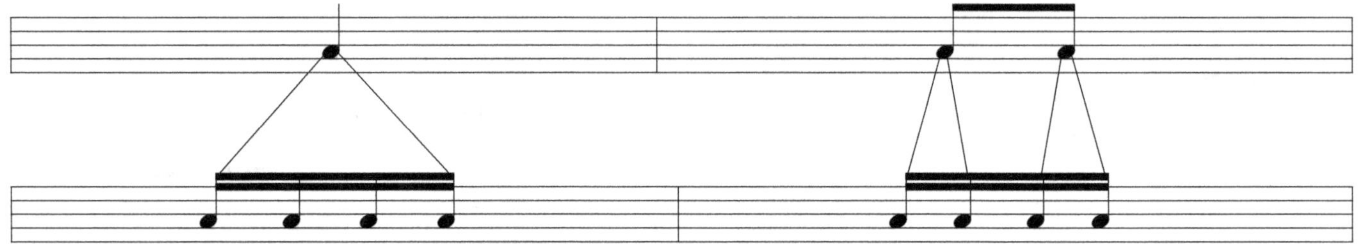

Music Rhythm Tree

Each example below shows how many of each note it takes to fill a measure. The La's indicate how to sing each note. If you see "La - - -" that means you are holding the note for more than one beat.

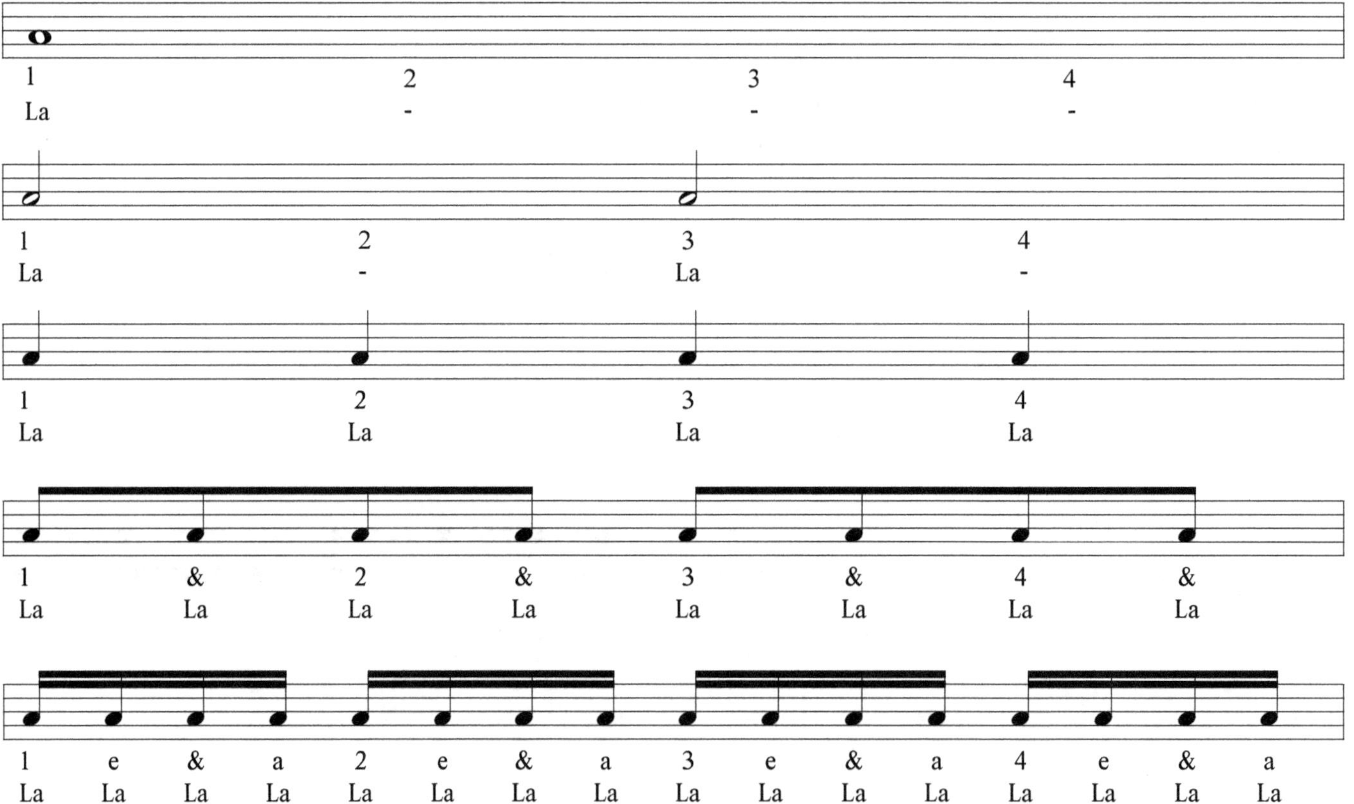

Review: Lesson 2

1. Check the correct counting for each of these examples.

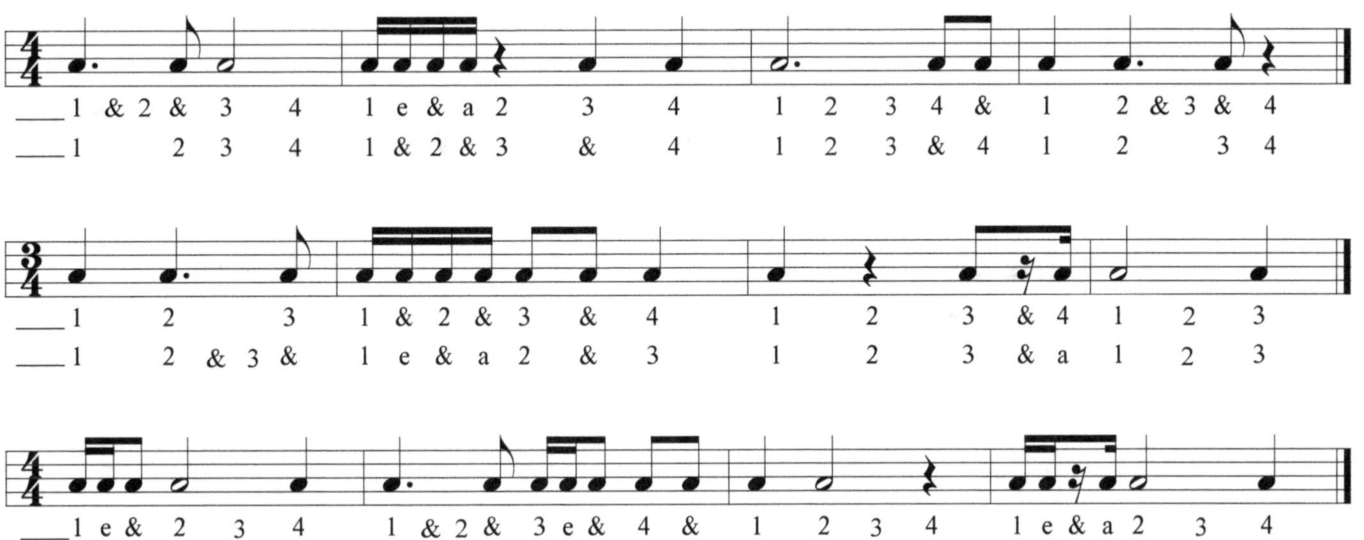

2. Check the correct number of beats each note or rest will receive in $\frac{4}{4}$ time.

3. Circle the correct name for each note or rest.

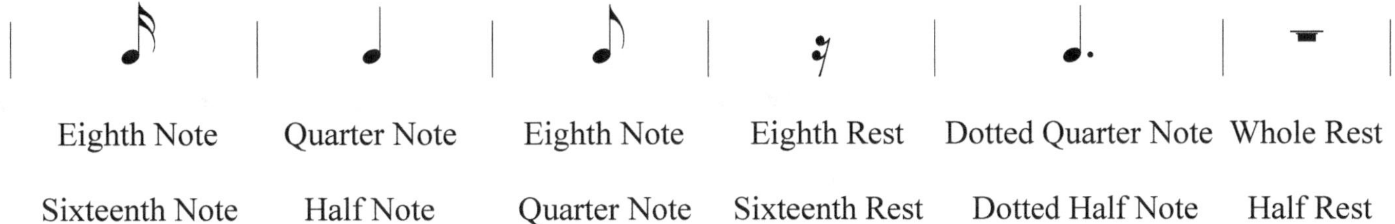

4. Write the beats under the notes, then add missing bar lines and a double bar line to each example.

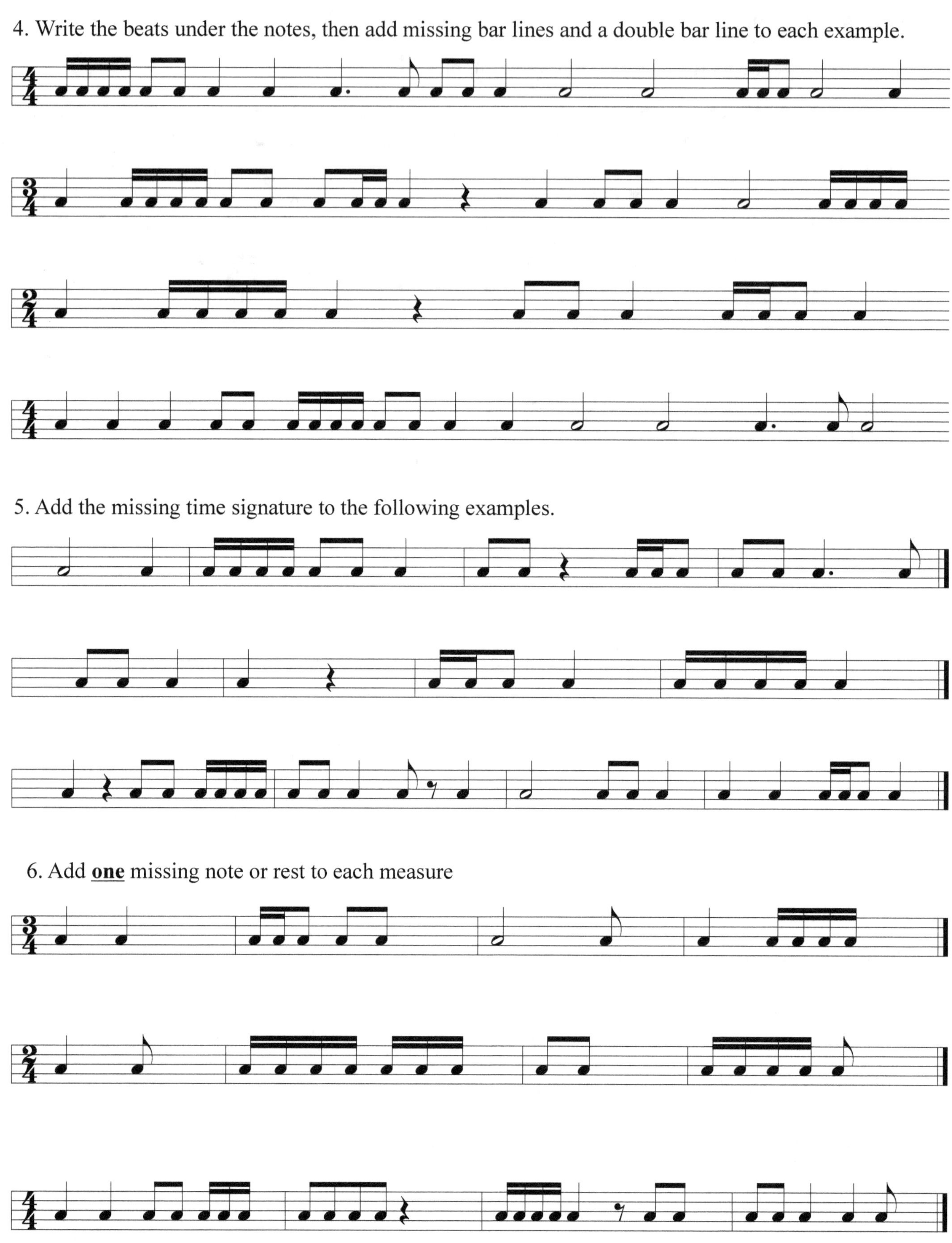

5. Add the missing time signature to the following examples.

6. Add **one** missing note or rest to each measure

7. Write the beats under the notes/rests in each example, then write La's according to how you would sing the notes. You can use dashes to indicate held notes. The first example is done for you.

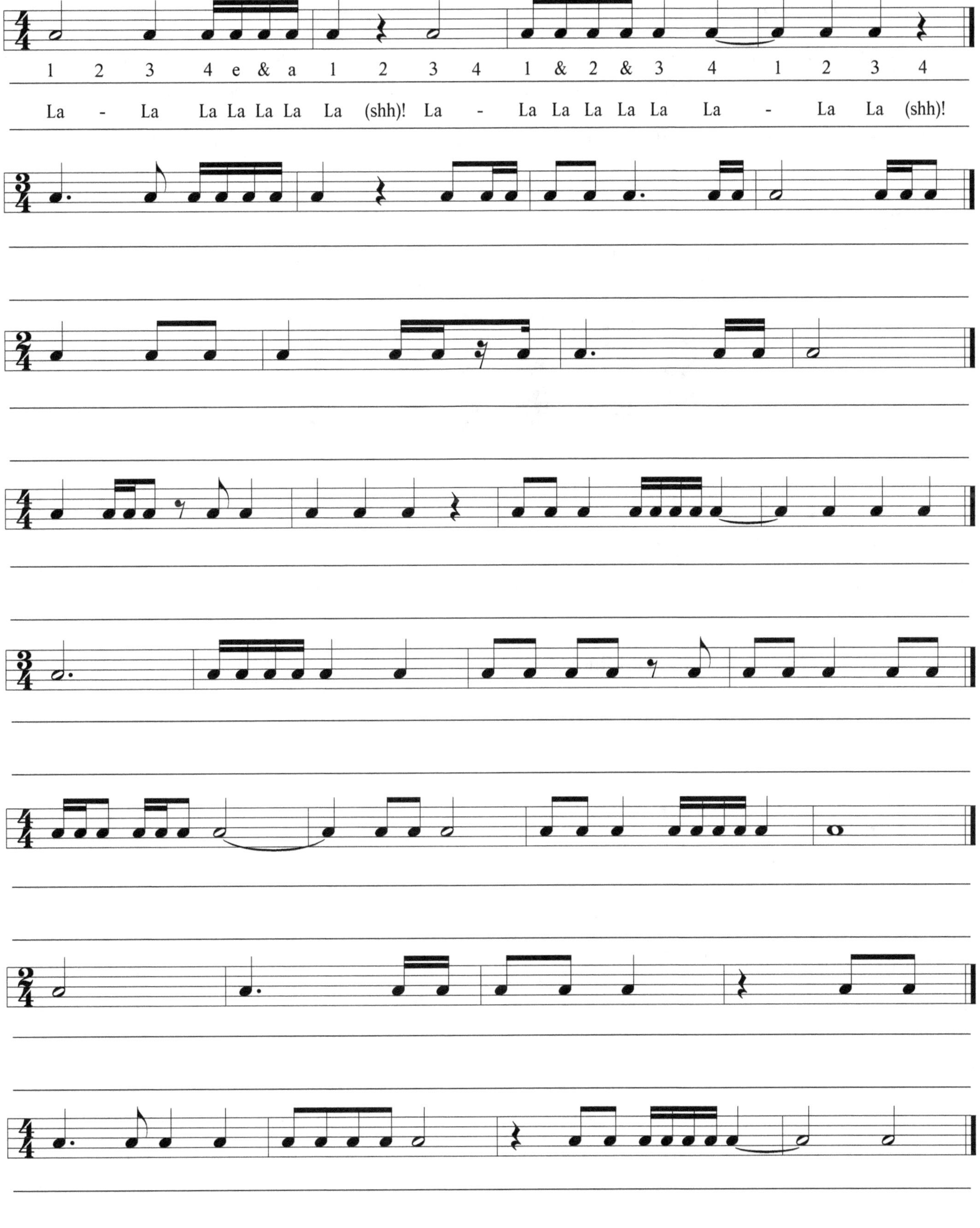

Lesson 3: Key Signatures

In music, a Key Signature is a series of sharp (♯) or flat (♭) symbols placed on the staff immediately after the Treble and Bass clefs.

The Key Signature shows which notes are to be sung a half step higher (sharp) or a half step lower (flat) for the duration of the piece. The Key Signature also creates the tonal center for a piece.

For singers, in moveable Do (solfege), Do is the same as the Key Signature. For example, if a piece is in the key of G Major, Do is G.

Enharmonic Notes

An Enharmonic note (pitch) is a note that has two different names. For example, C♯ and D♭ are the same note/pitch, but called two different names. Look at the piano below to see the enharmonic notes.

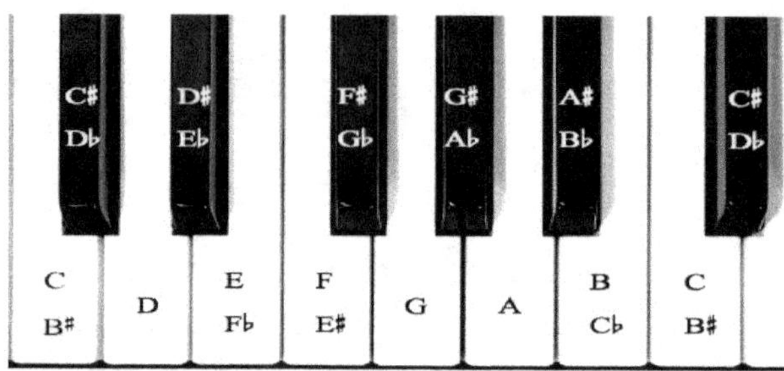

Enharmonic Key Signatures

Enharmonic Key Signatures share the same notes/pitches but have different names. They are grouped together below.

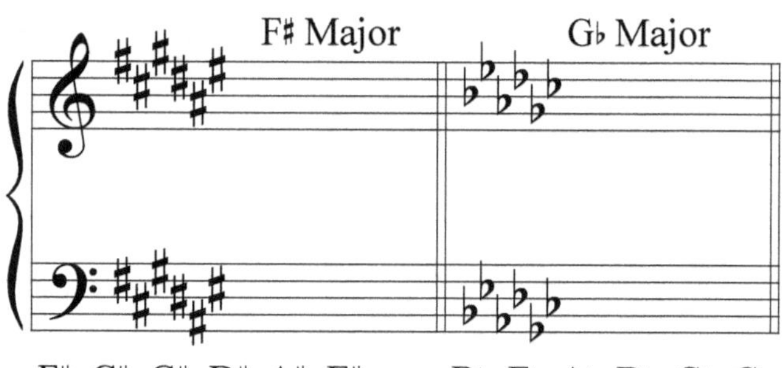

F♯, C♯, G♯, D♯, A♯, E♯   B♭, E♭, A♭, D♭, G♭, C♭

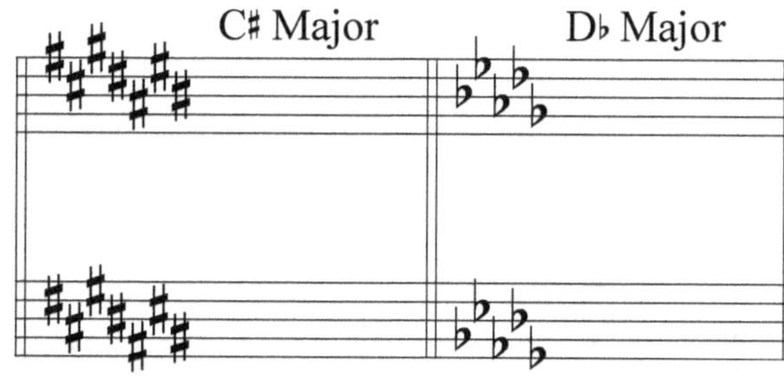

F♯, C♯, G♯, D♯, A♯, E♯, B♯ - B♭, E♭, A♭, D♭, G♭

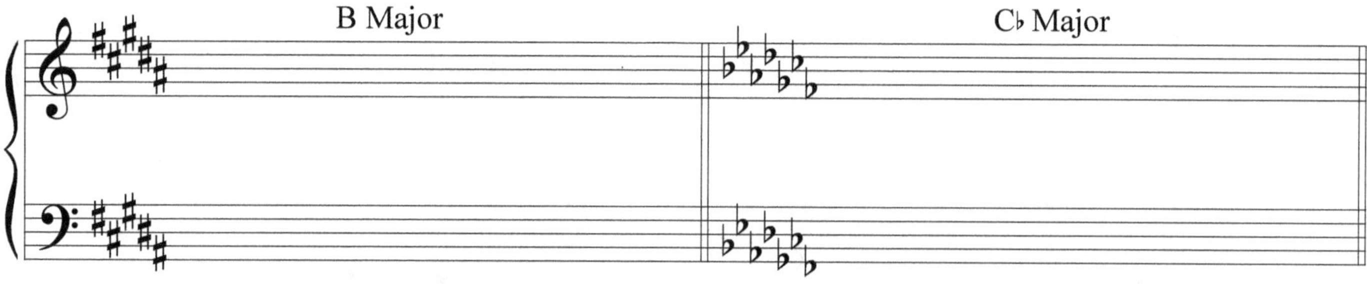

F♯, C♯, G♯, D♯, A♯   B♭, E♭, A♭, D♭, G♭, C♭, F♭

The following examples are written in enharmonic key signatures. The solfege and note names are written in. Try singing the examples so you can hear how "Do" sounds the same for the enharmonic keys. You can use the piano below to give yourself the starting pitch.

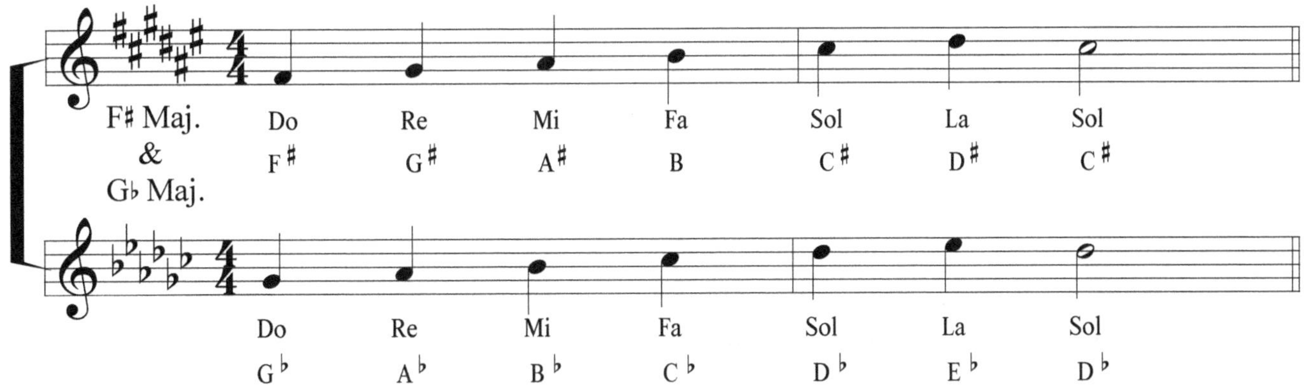

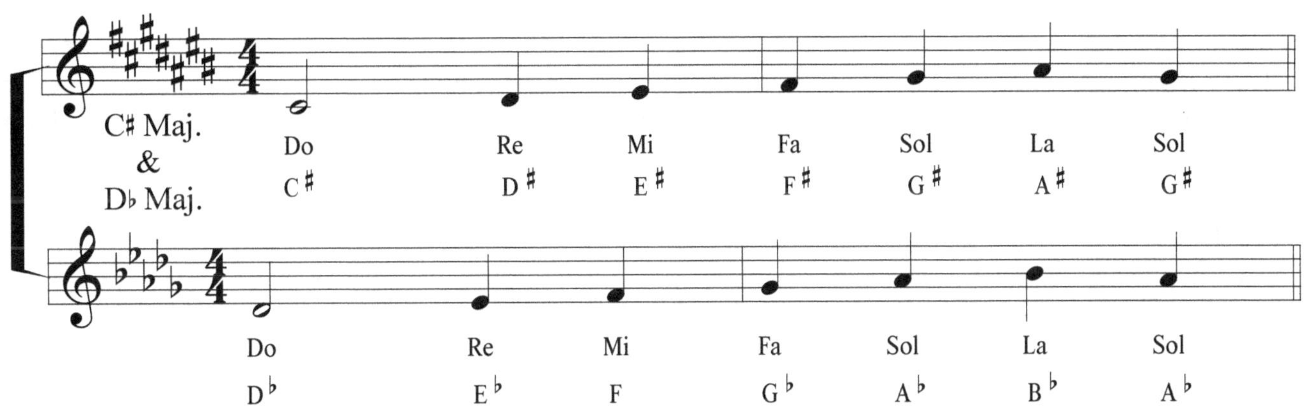

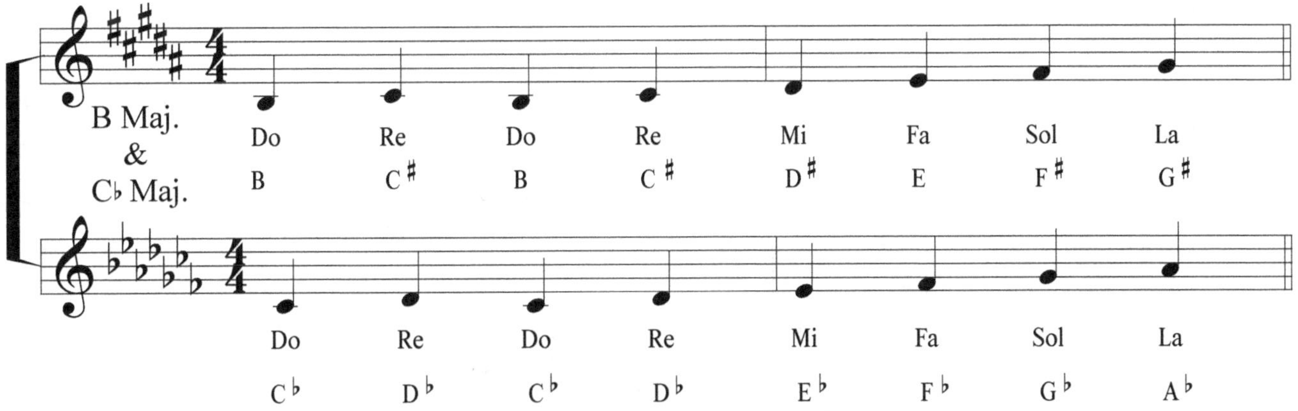

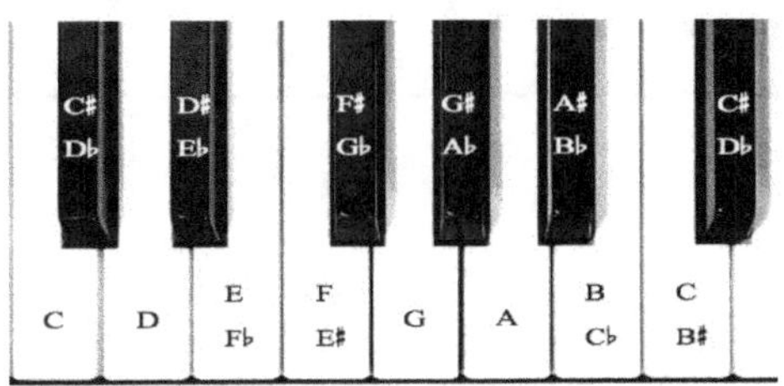

Sharp Key Signatures

♯ - The order of sharps in a key signature is: F, C, G, D, A, E, B. You can use the following saying to remember the order of the sharps: **F**at **C**ats **G**o **D**own **A**lleys **E**ating **B**urritos.

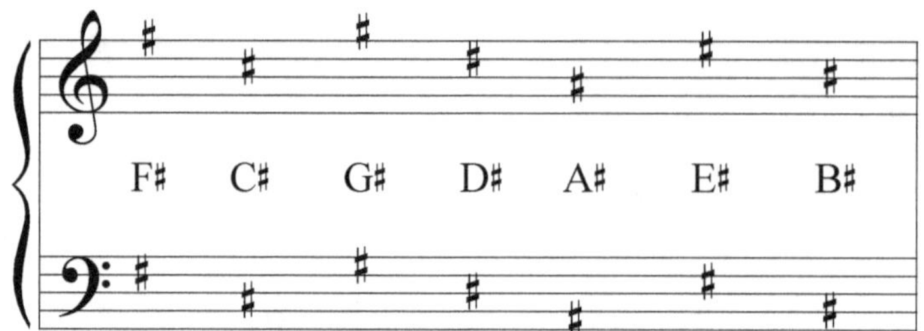

In order to tell what key a song is in (how many sharps it has) look at the **last sharp** (furthest to the right) then **name the next letter in the musical alphabet** (or name the next note 1/2 step up). That's the key.

You can also think of the last sharp (furthest to the right) as "Ti" in the Major scale. The next note up is "Do" which is the key.

In the example below, there are four sharps (F♯, C♯, G♯ & D♯). The last sharp is D♯. The next letter in the musical alphabet (or the next note 1/2 step up from D♯) is E. Therefore, the key signature is E Major.

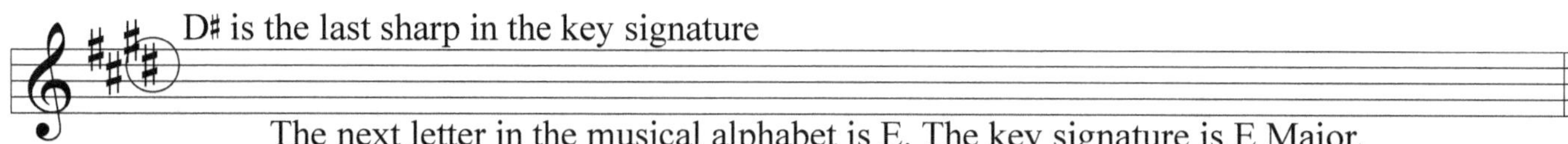

Remember, there are two key signatures with a ♯ in their name (F♯ and C♯). So, for example,when E♯ is the last sharp in the key signature, the next note 1/2 step up is an F♯, not just an F. Look at the examples (staff & keyboard) below.

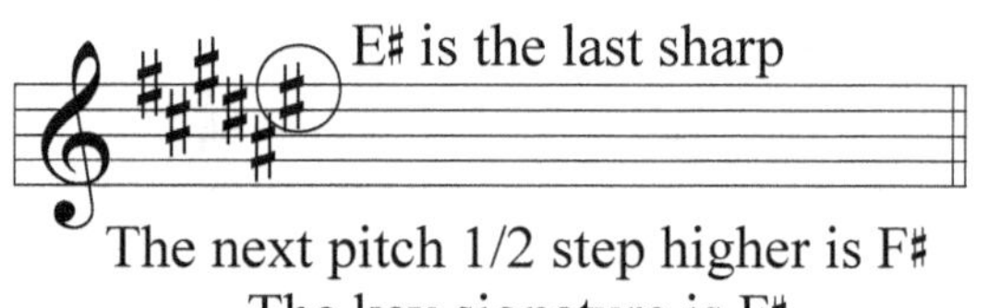

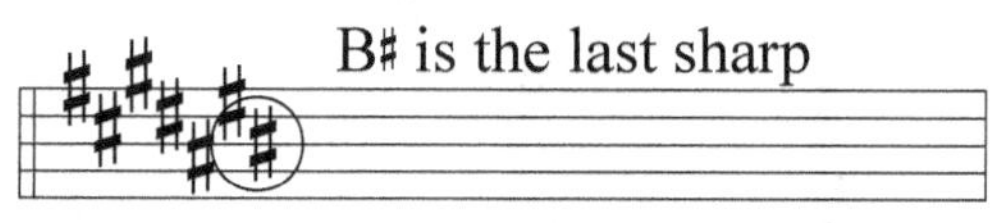

The next pitch 1/2 step higher is C♯
The key signature is C♯

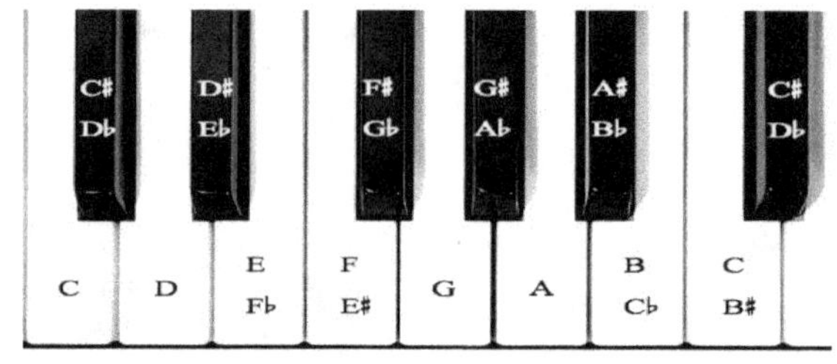

If you are asked to name the sharps in a key signature, name the musical alphabet letter before the key and all the sharps before it. For example:

Question: How many sharps are in B Major?

Answer: The musical alphabet letter before B is A, so the sharps in the key of B are:
F♯, C♯, G♯, D♯ and A♯.

Question: How many sharps are in A Major? (this one is a little confusing, because in our regular alphabet, there are no letters before A, but in the musical alphabet, a G is before A (ABCDEFGABCDEFG).

Answer: The musical alphabet letter before A is G, so the sharps in the key of A are:
F♯, C♯, and G♯.

Here are the Major Sharp Key Signatures, with their sharps listed below.

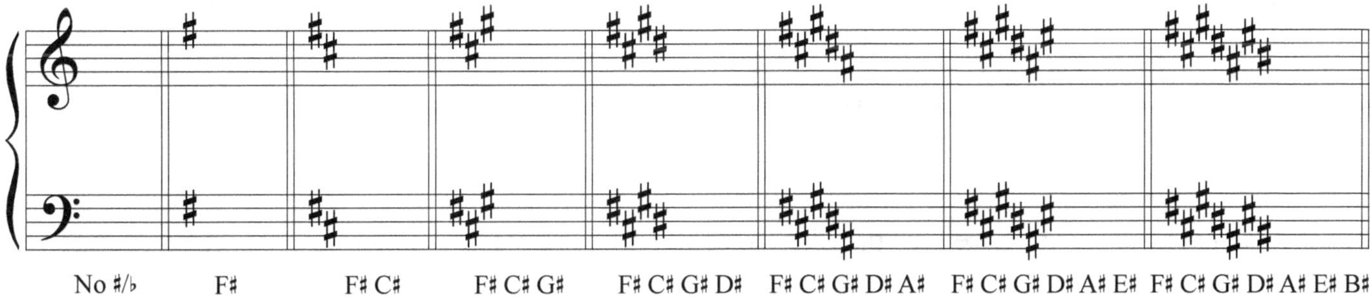

Here are the names of the Major Sharp Key Signatures. (C is also included)

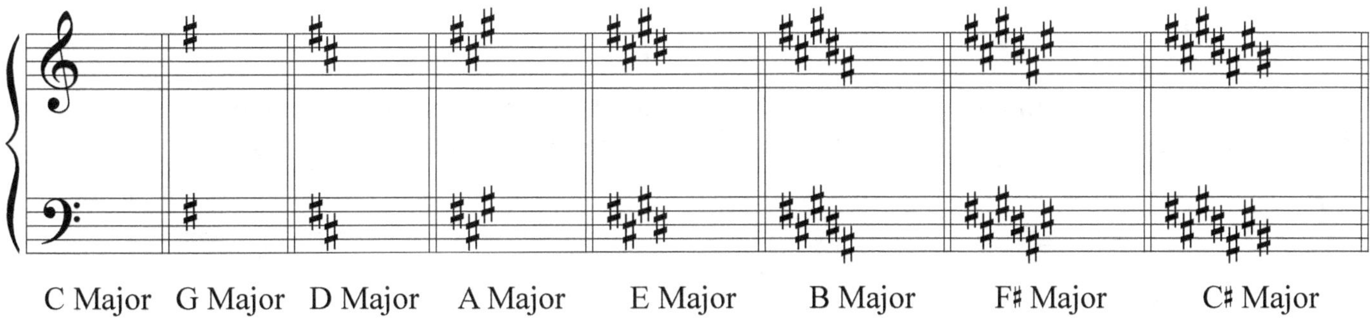

*Notice how sharp key signature are named as an alphabet letter, G, D, A, E, B-except for F♯ & C♯.

Flat Key Signatures

♭ - The order of flats in a key signature is: B, E, A, D, G, C, F. You can use the following saying to remember the order of the flats: **BEAD**- **G**um **C**andy **F**ruit.

The order of flats also happens to be in the opposite order of the sharps.

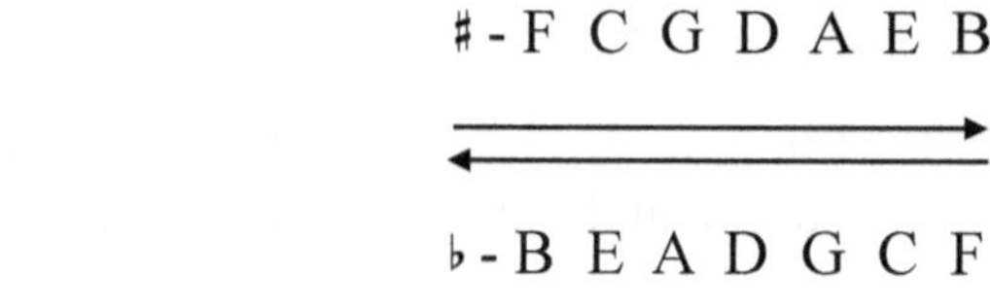

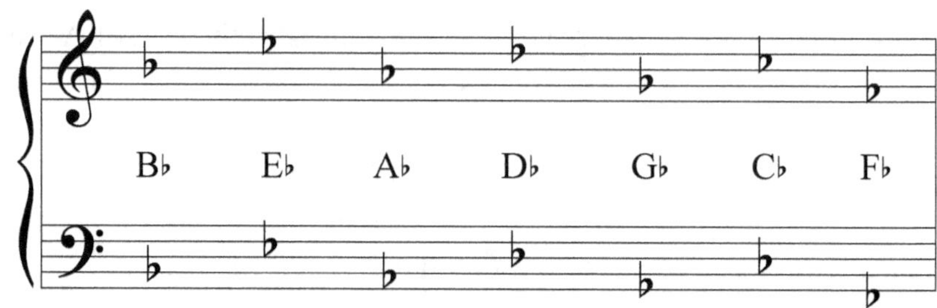

In order to tell what key a song is in (how many flats it has) look at the **second to the last flat** and that's the key.

You can also think of the last flat (farthest to the right) as "Fa" of the Major scale. If you count up from Fa to Do, you will also find the key.

In the example below, there are four flats. The second to the last flat is A♭, therefore the key signature is A♭ Major.

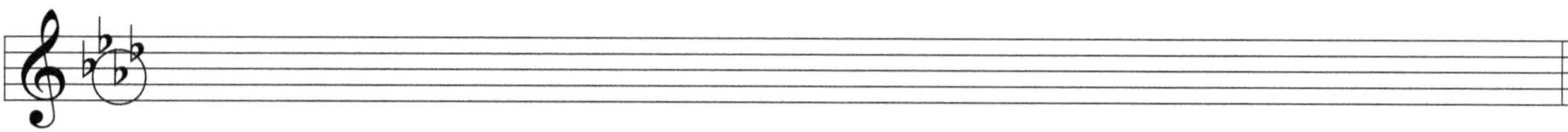

A♭ - This is the second to the last flat, so it is the key.

The only key this rule will not work for is F Major. It only has one flat, so there is no second to the last flat for you to find. You will need to memorize the key signature for F Major.

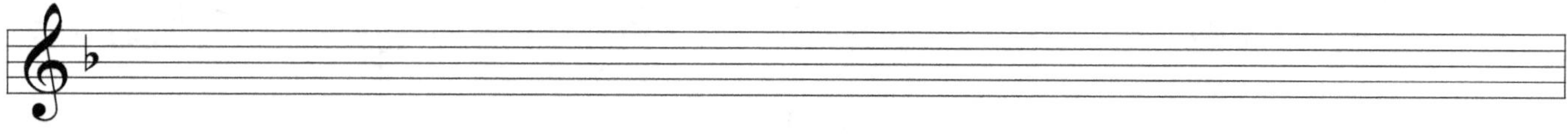

F Major

If you are asked to name the flats in a key, name the musical alphabet letter before the key, then add one more. For example:

Question: How many flats are in the key of G♭?

Answer: G♭ is the second to the last flat in the key signature, so the flats in the key of G♭ Major are: B♭, E♭, A♭, D♭, G♭ and C♭.

Question: How many flats are in the key of B♭?

Answer: B♭ is the second to the last flat in the key signature, so the flats in the key of B♭ Major are: B♭ and E♭.

Here are the Major Flat Key Signatures, with their flats listed below.

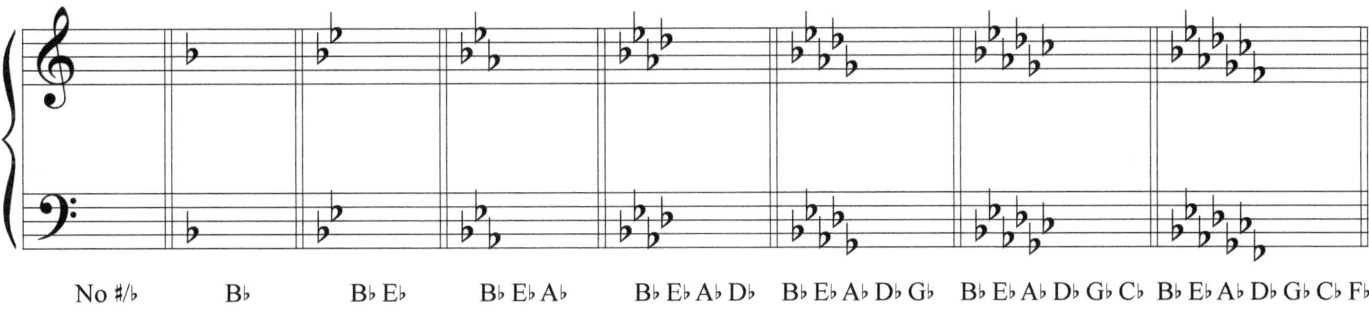

Here are the **names** of the Major Flat Key Signatures (C is also included).

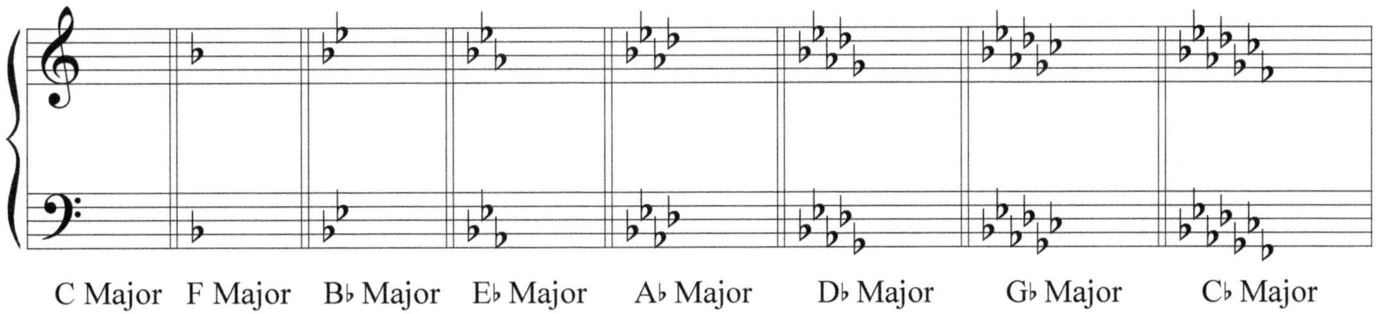

*Fun fact: C Major has no ♯/♭ - C♯ Major has all 7 sharps - C♭ Major has all of the flats!

Review: Lesson 3

Check the correct answer for the following questions.

1. Enharmonic means:
   ___two different notes sung at the same time
   ___a note/pitch that has two different names but sounds the same

2. The enharmonic note for F♯ is:
   ___G♭
   ___F♭

3. The enharmonic note for C♭ is:
   ___C♯
   ___B

4. The enharmonic key for G♭ is:
   ___F♯
   ___G

5. The enharmonic key for C♯ is:
   ___D♭
   ___C

Answer the following questions about key signatures.

6. What is the order of sharps in a key signature?

___ ___ ___ ___ ___ ___ ___

7. What saying can be used to remember the order of sharps?

____

8. What is the order of flats in a key signature?

___ ___ ___ ___ ___ ___ ___

9. What saying can be used to remember the order of flats?

____

10. The order of sharps is in the ____________________ order than the order of flats.

11. Draw the sharps 3 times, in order, on both the treble and bass staves. Be careful that the center part of the sharp is on the correct line or space. Refer to pages 14 or 15 for help.

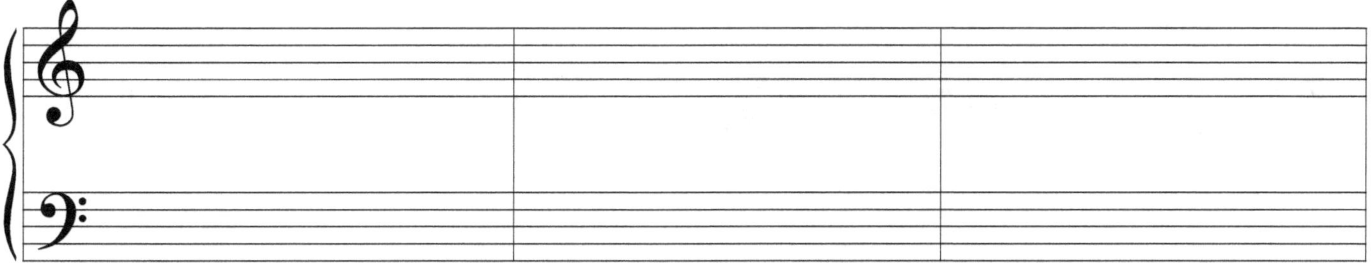

12. Draw the flats 3 times, in order, on both the treble and bass staves. Be careful that the center part of the flat is on the correct line or space. Refer to pages 16 or 17 for help.

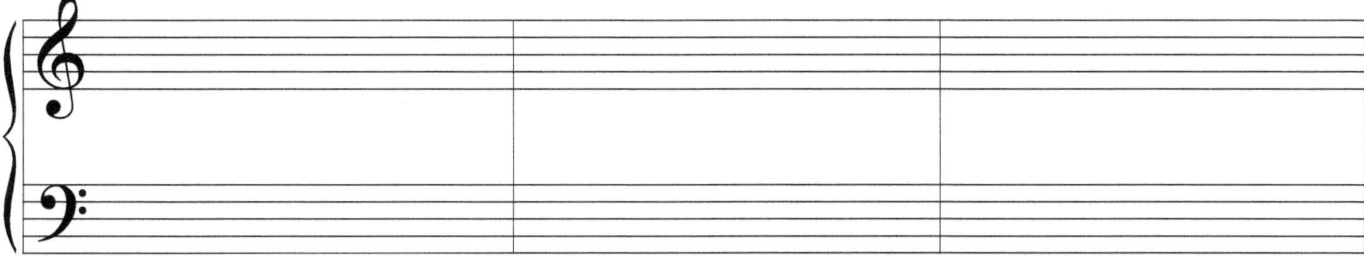

13. Add sharps (♯) or flats (♭) to complete each of these Major scales.

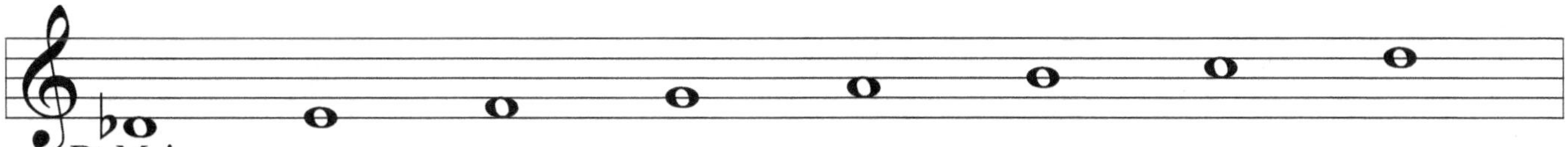

D♭ Major

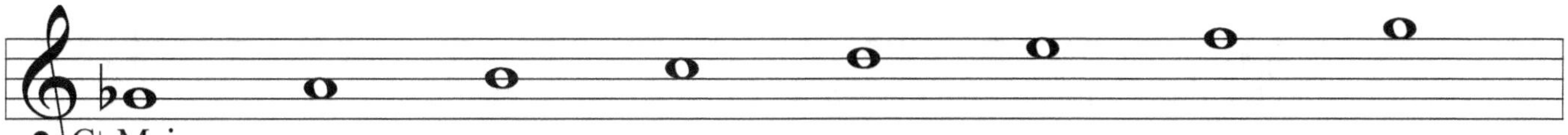

G♭ Major

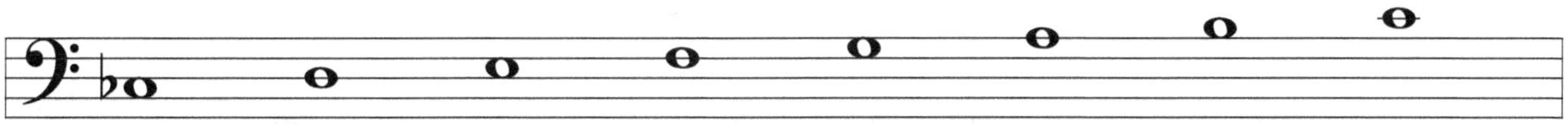

C♭ Major

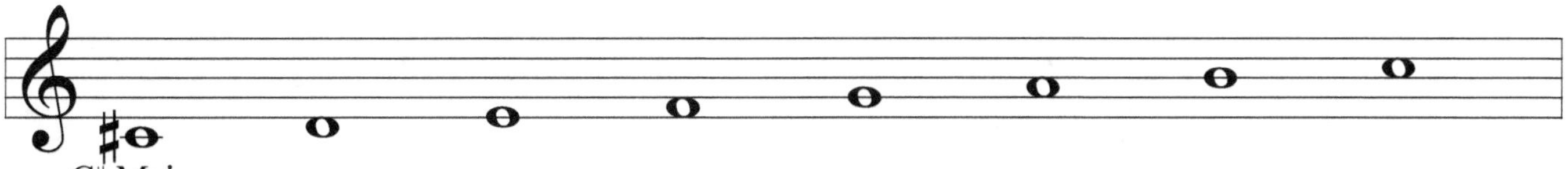

C♯ Major

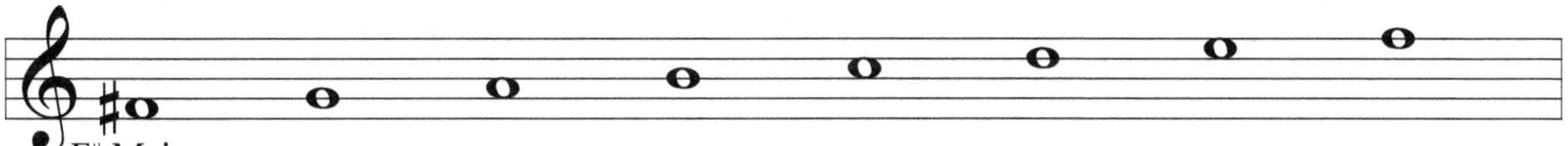

F♯ Major

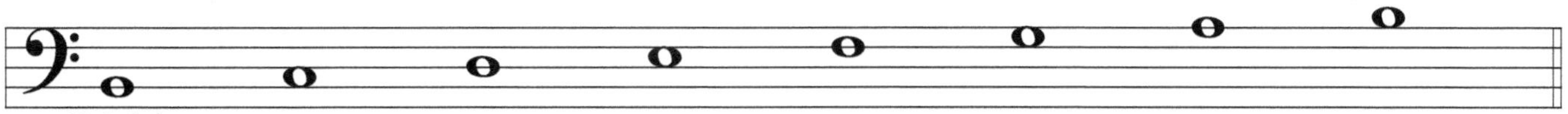

B Major

14. Name the sharps, in order, in the following keys. Make sure to add a ♯ after the alphabet letter. You may want to write the order of the sharps at the top of this page so you can refer to it. The first one is done for you.

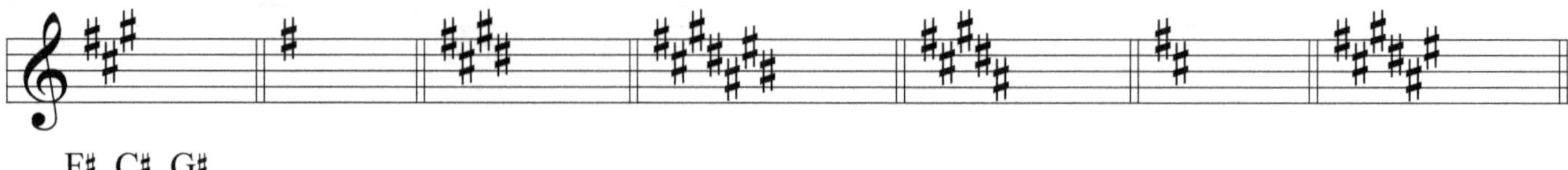

F♯, C♯, G♯

15. Name the flats, in order in the following keys. Make sure to add a ♭ after the alphabet letter. You may want to write the order of the flats at the top of this page so you can refer to it. The first one is done for you.

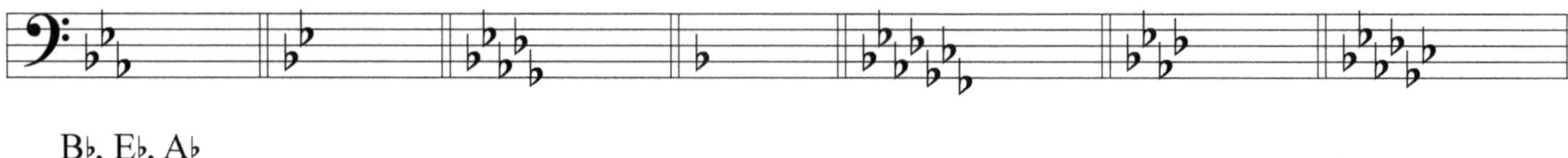

B♭, E♭, A♭

16. Name the following Major key signatures. Don't forget to add a ♯ if necessary. The first one is done for you.

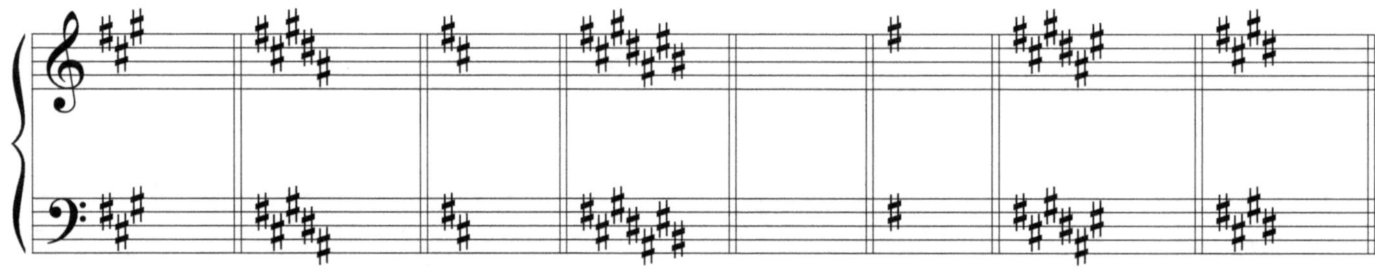

A Major

17. Name the following Major key signatures. Don't forget to add a ♭ if necessary. The first one is done for you.

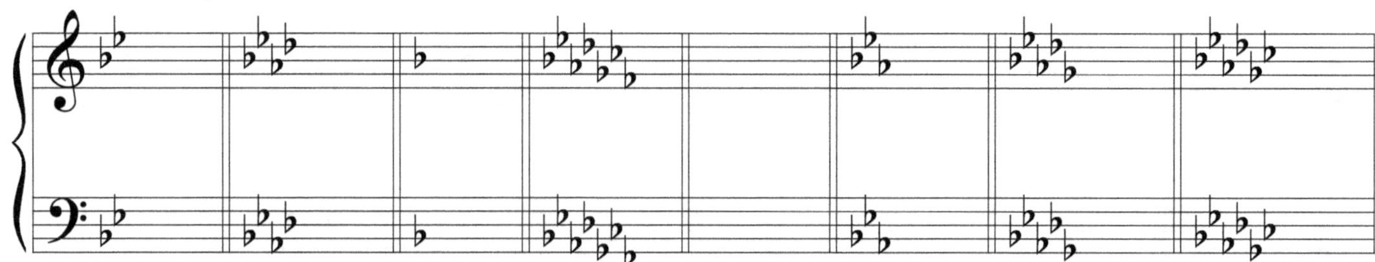

B♭ Major

18. For the following examples:
   - Circle the notes affected by the key signature.
   - Write the note names underneath the notes. Be sure to add the ♯/♭ if the note is affected by the key signature. Watch the clef changes- it may help to circle the Bass clefs so you don't forget! The first measure is done for you.

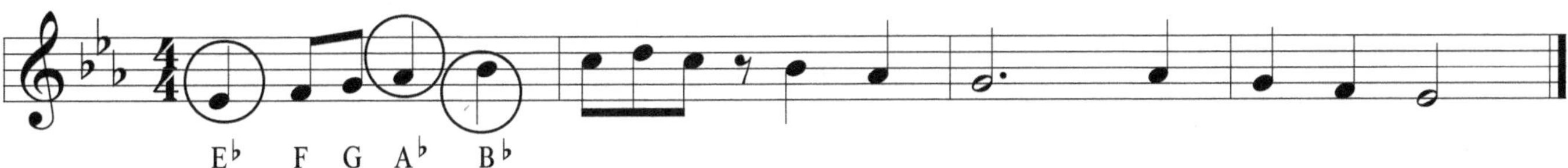

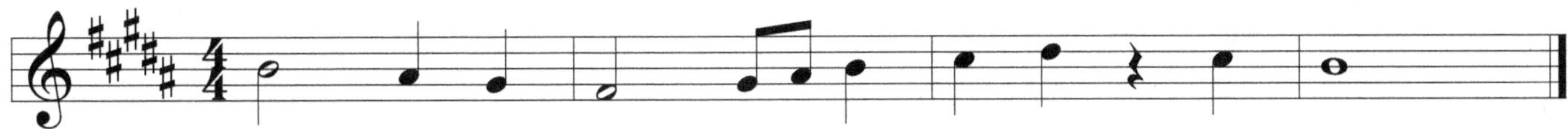

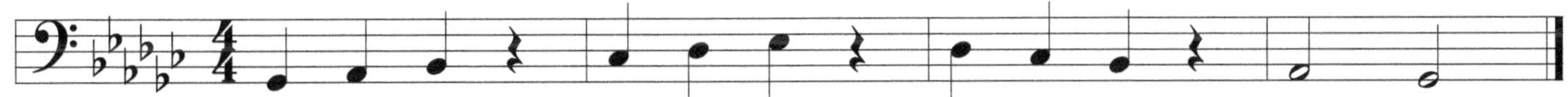

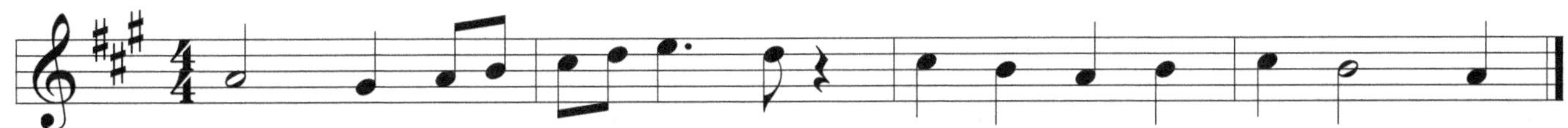

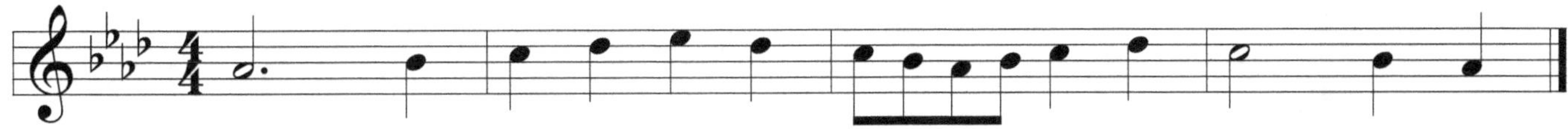

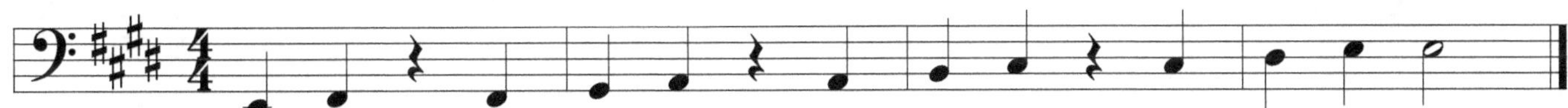

Lesson 4: Triads

A **Triad**, or 3-note chord, is formed when the first, third and fifth notes of a scale are sung or played, either consecutively or at the same time. The root, or the lowest note of a triad, determines its letter name.

Example G♭ Major G♭ is the 1st/root, B♭ is the 3rd/middle note, D♭ is the 5th/top note

This is a "root position" chord.

The following examples show the Major Scales and Major Triads formed on the first note of the scale (Do). The 1st, 3rd, and 5th notes (Do-Mi-Sol) are circled.

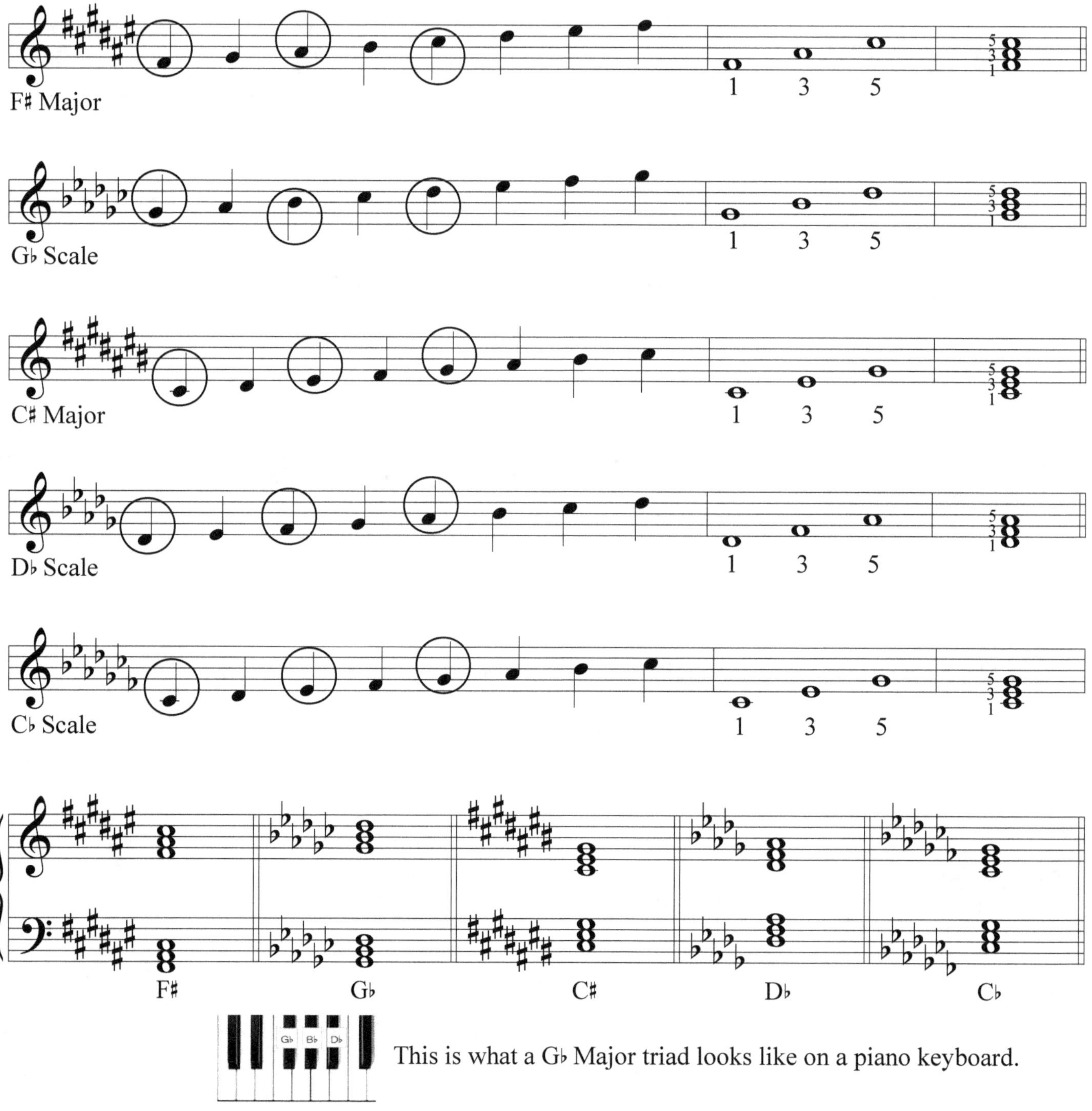

This is what a G♭ Major triad looks like on a piano keyboard.

Review: Lesson 4

1. Name the following triads. Remember, look at the bottom note (root) for the "name" of the triad.

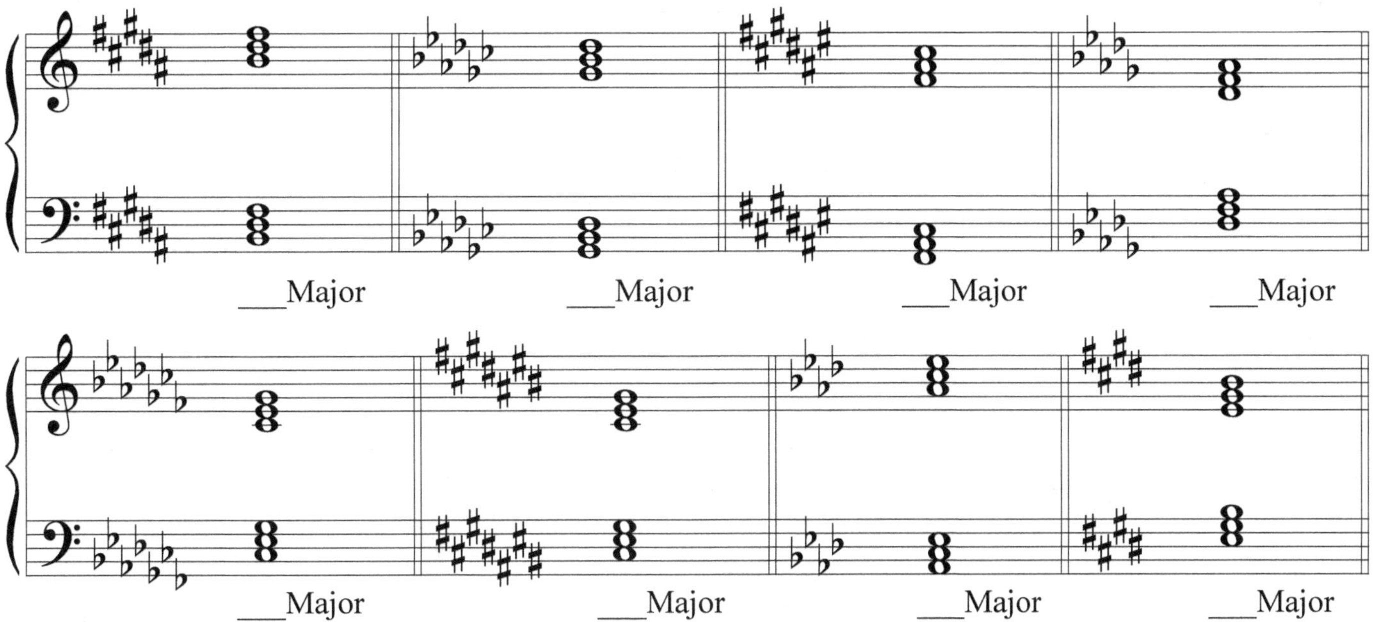

2. For the following examples, draw the correct key signature, then add the root position triads to both the Treble and Bass clefs. Look at question 1 for hints.

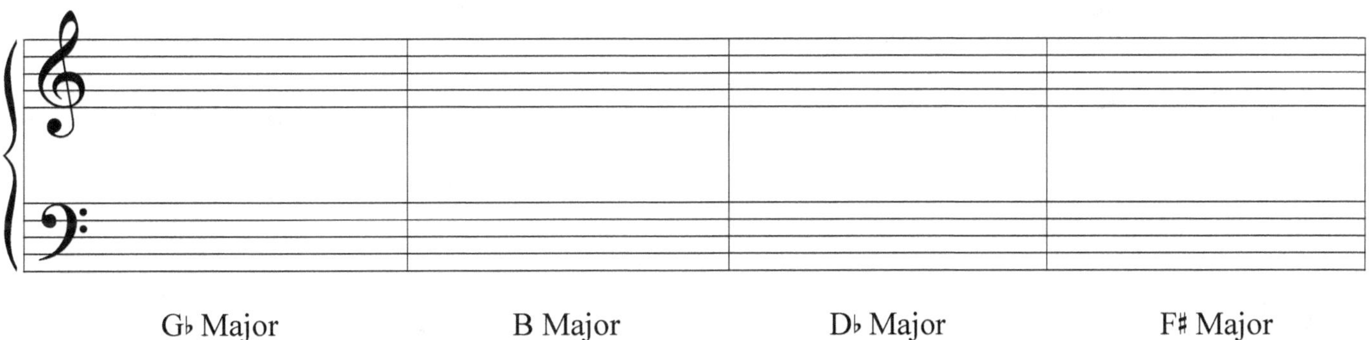

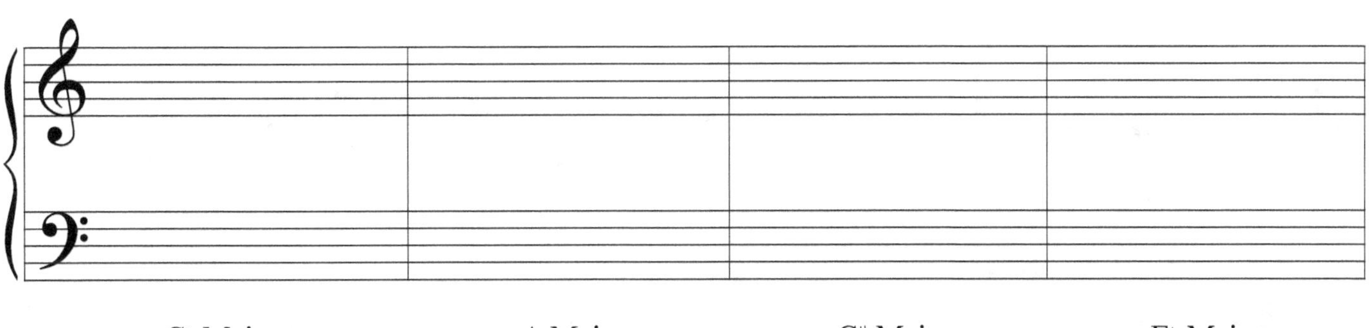

3. Circle the three notes in the scales below that make up a root position triad.

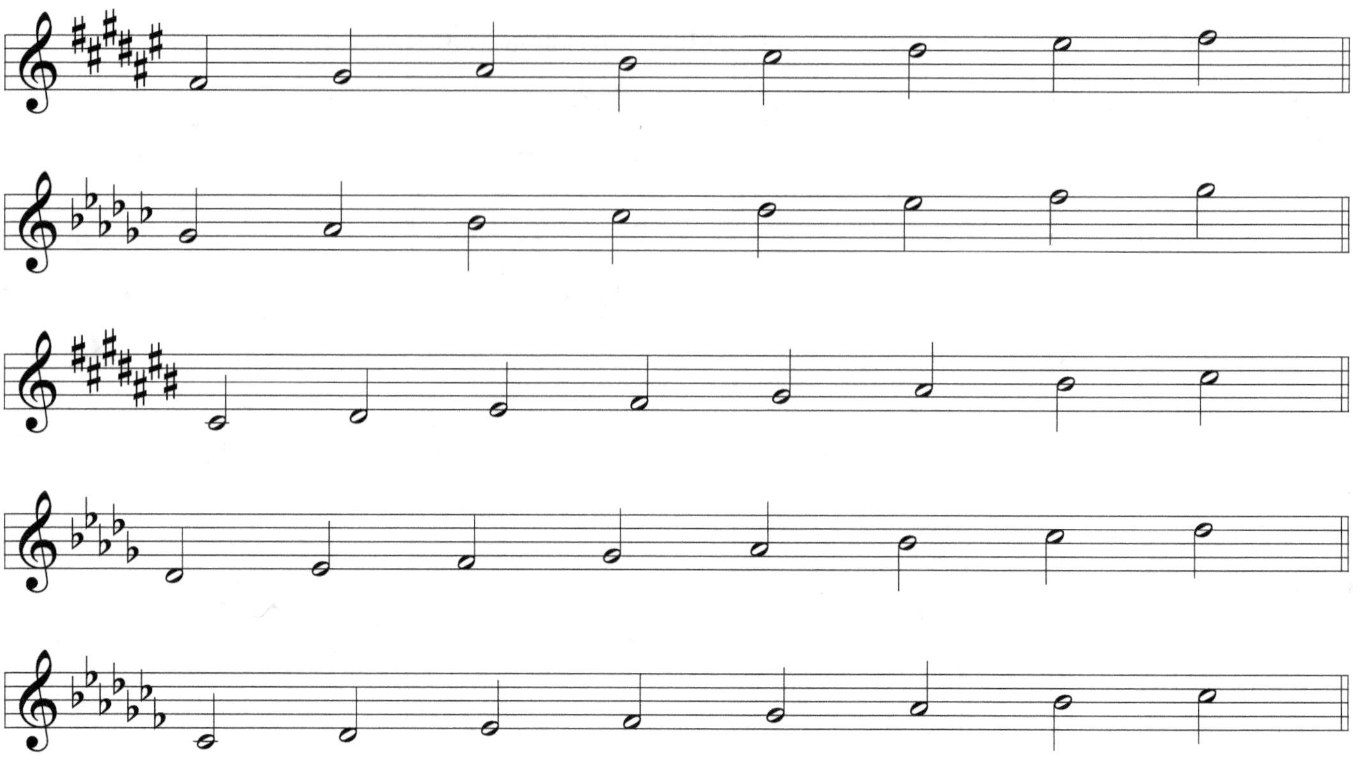

4. Each of these triads should have 3 notes (Do-Mi-Sol/root-middle-top).
Fill in the missing note to create a root position triad for the given key.

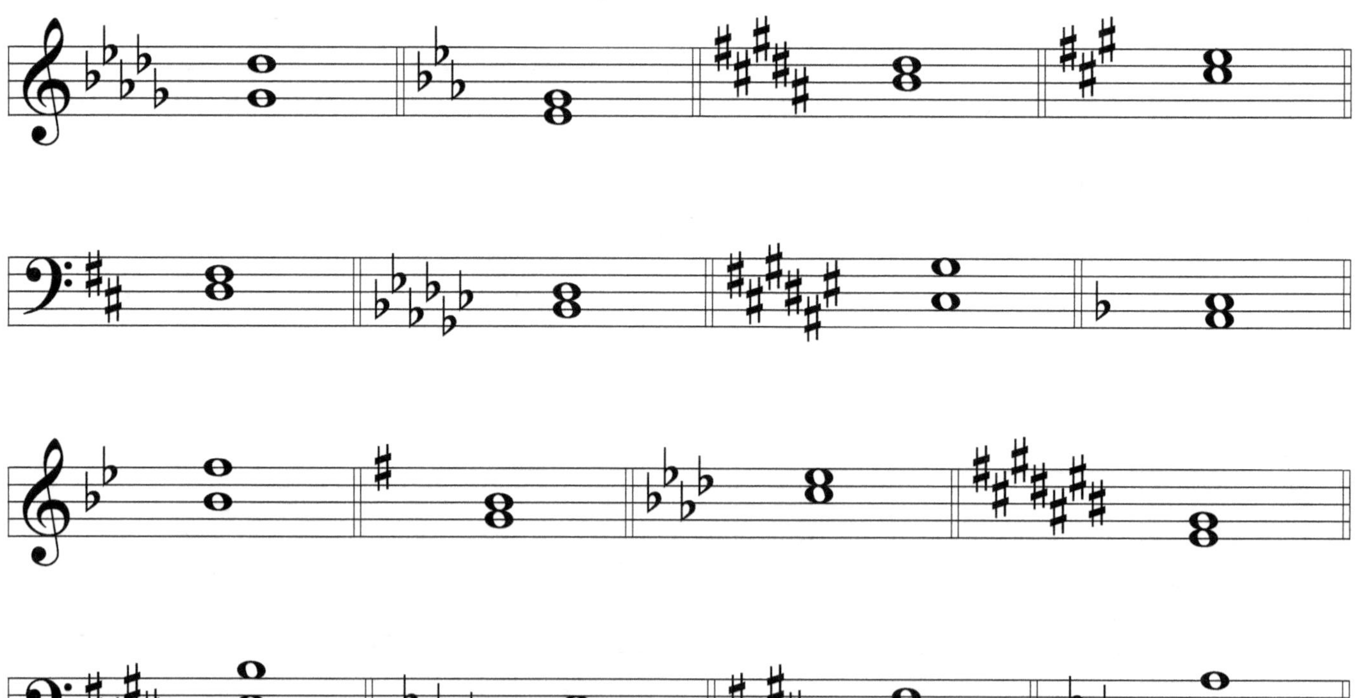

Review: Lessons 1-4

1. Draw the note a half step **higher** then the one given. Use half notes. Pay attention to the key signatures

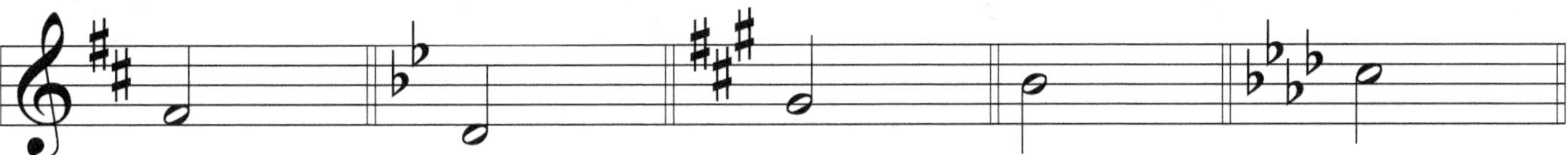

2. Draw the note a whole step **higher** then the one given. Use half notes.

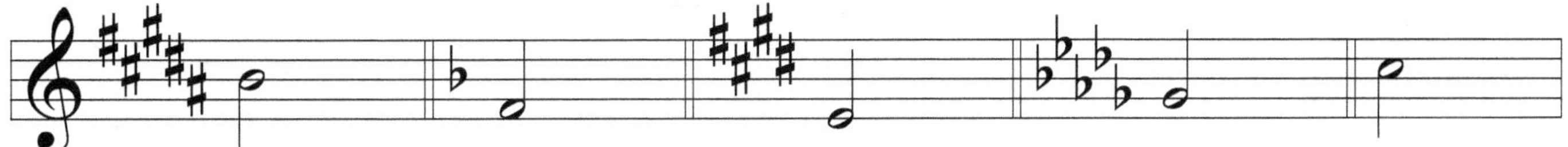

3. Draw the note a half step **lower** then the one given. Use quarter notes.

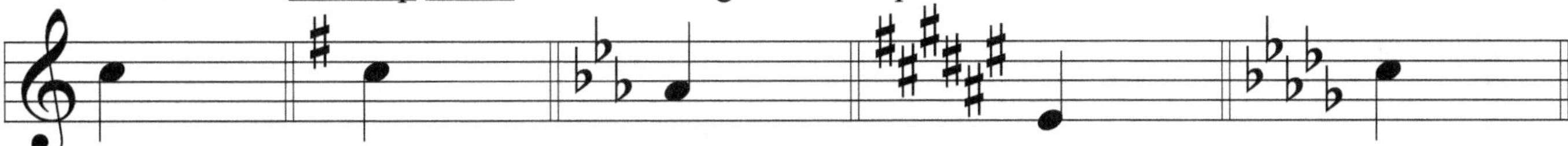

4. Draw the note a whole step **lower** then the one given. Use quarter notes.

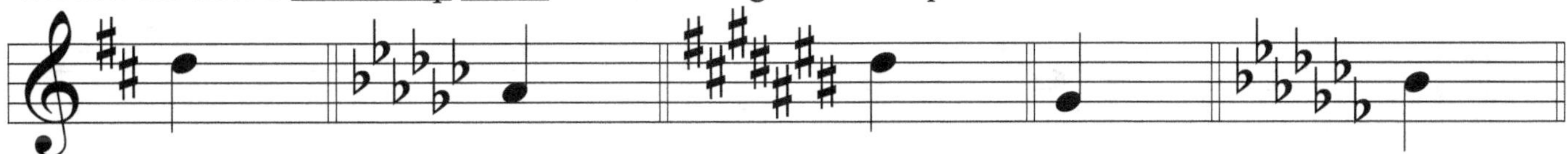

5. Name the note/rest and how many beats it has.

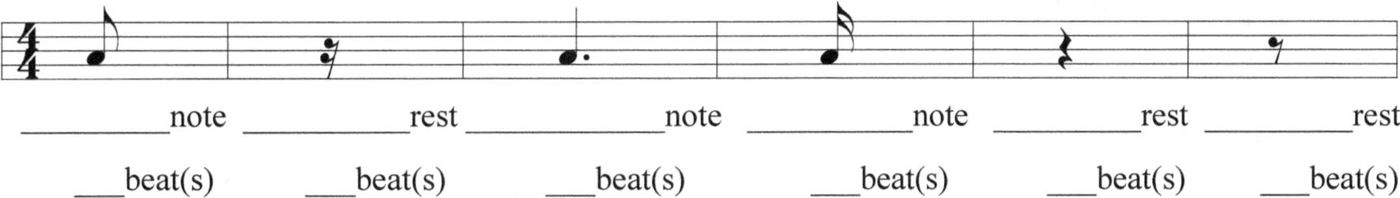

6. Check the correct counting for the example below.

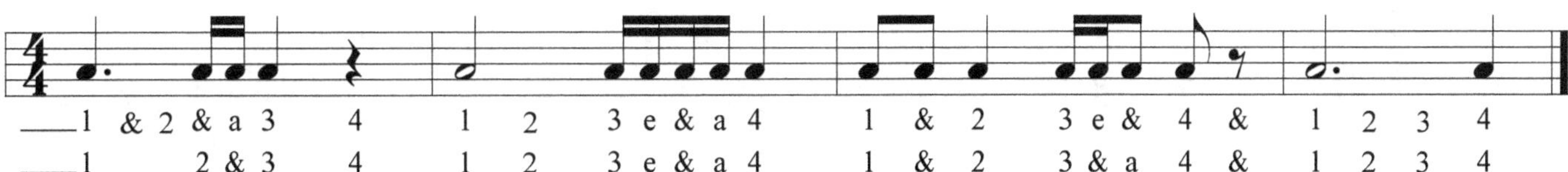

7. Write the beats under each note/rest in the following example.

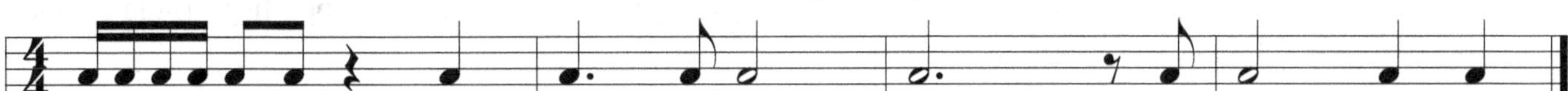

8. Add the 3 missing bar lines and a double bar line to the example below.

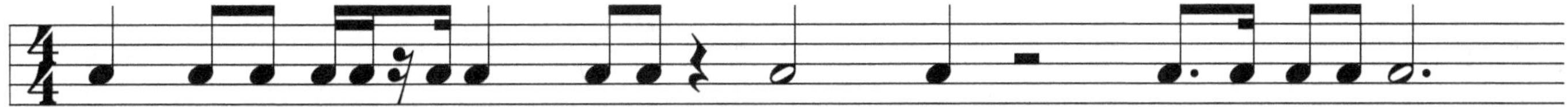

9. Add **one** missing note or rest to complete each measure in the example below.

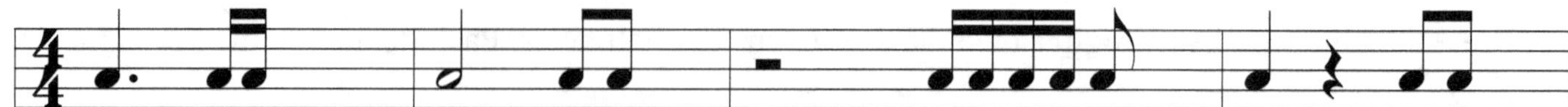

10. Add the necessary ♯/♭'s to the scales below to create Major scales.

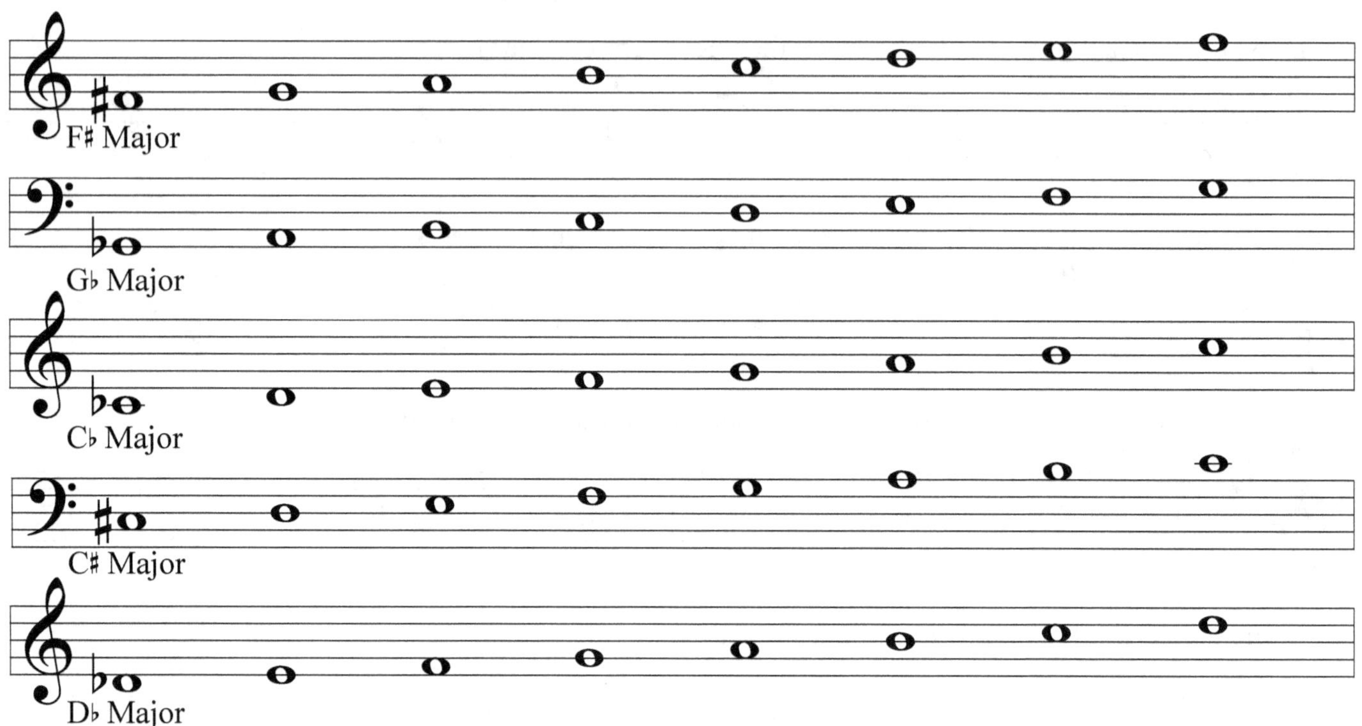

11. Name the following triads. Remember, look at the bottom note (root) for the "name" of the triad.

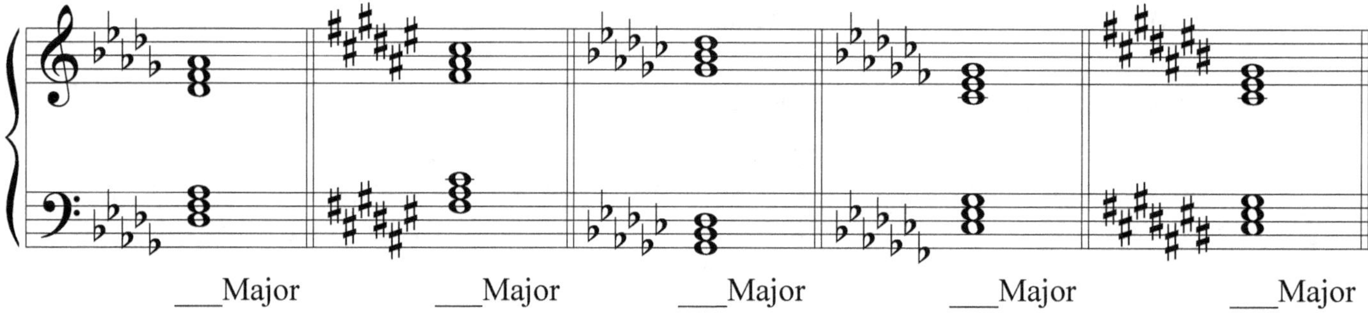

12. For the following examples, draw the correct key signature, then add the root position triads to both the Treble and Bass clefs. Look at question 11 for hints.

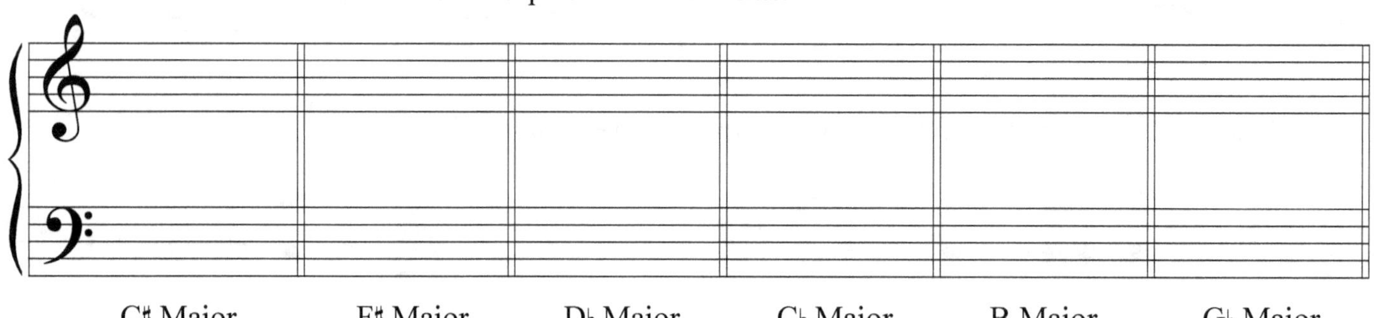

13. Circle the three notes in the scale below that make up a root position triad.

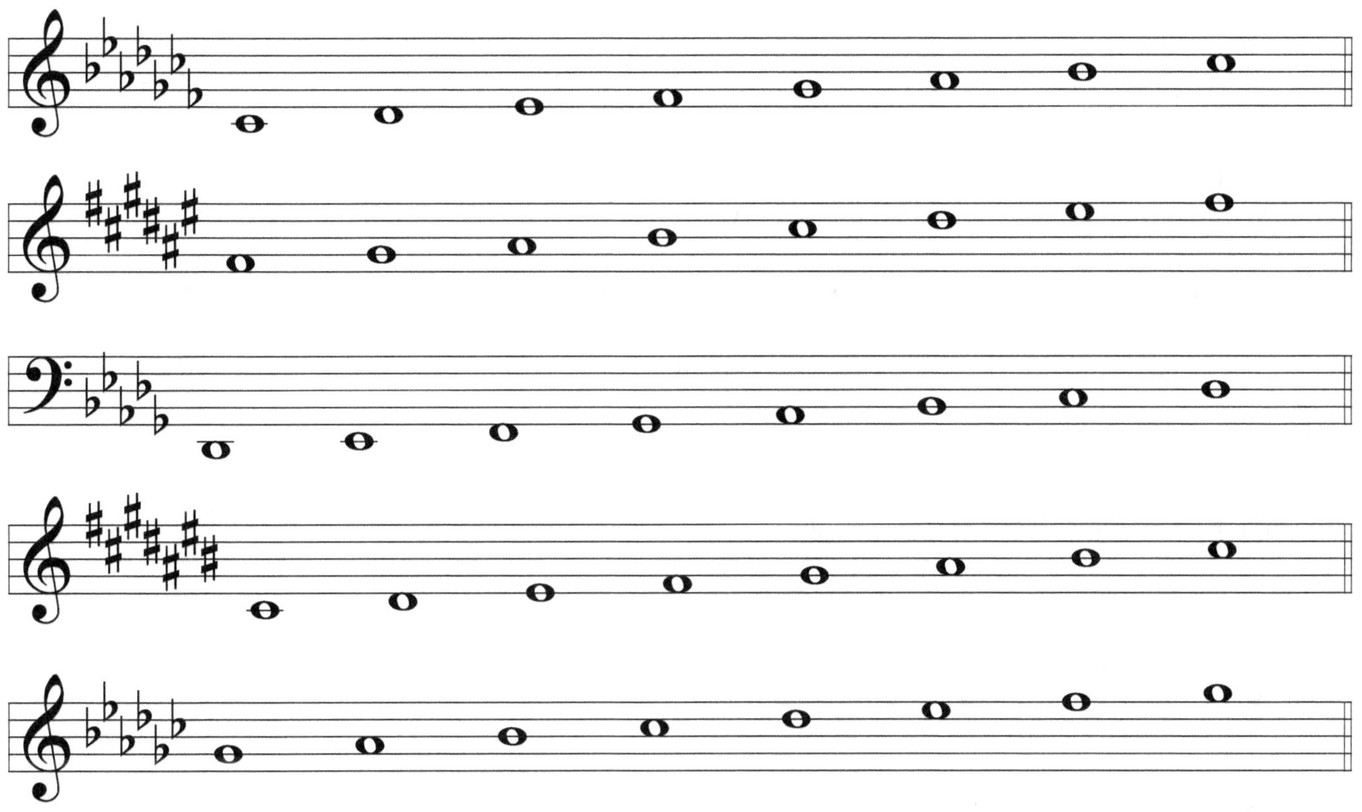

14. Each of these triads should have 3 notes (Do-Mi-Sol/root-middle-top). First, determine the key, then fill in the missing note to create a root position triad for the given key.

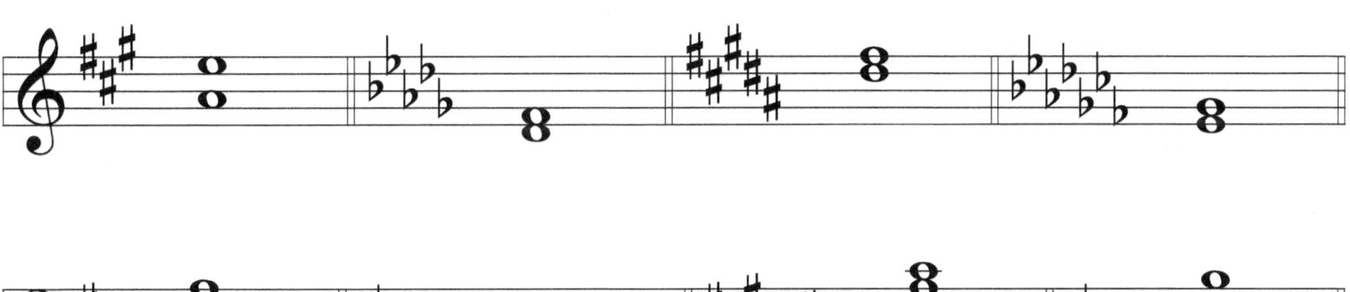

Lesson 5: Intervals (8th/Octave)

An Interval in music, is the distance between any two notes. In this level, the interval of an octave (8th) will be covered. The intervals of a 2nd, 3rd, 4th, 5th, 6th & 7th were covered in Levels 1-3.
When counting intervals, be sure to include the bottom and top notes.

For singing, Do-Do is an 8th, also called an octave. Intervals are sung melodically (one note at a time), or harmonically (two notes at the same time - two singers singing at the same time).

Look at the examples below. Notice how the interval of an octave has a line and a space note.

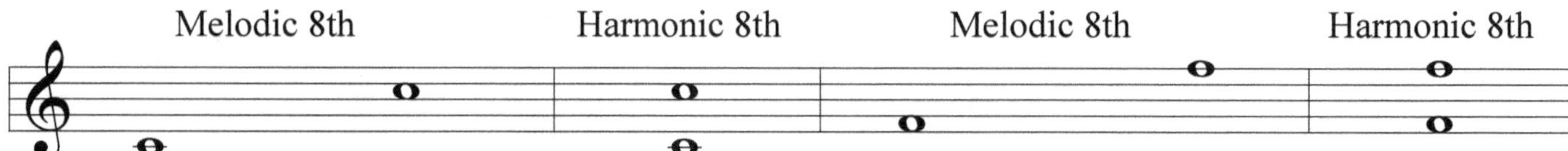

In singing, the Major intervals use the following solfege:

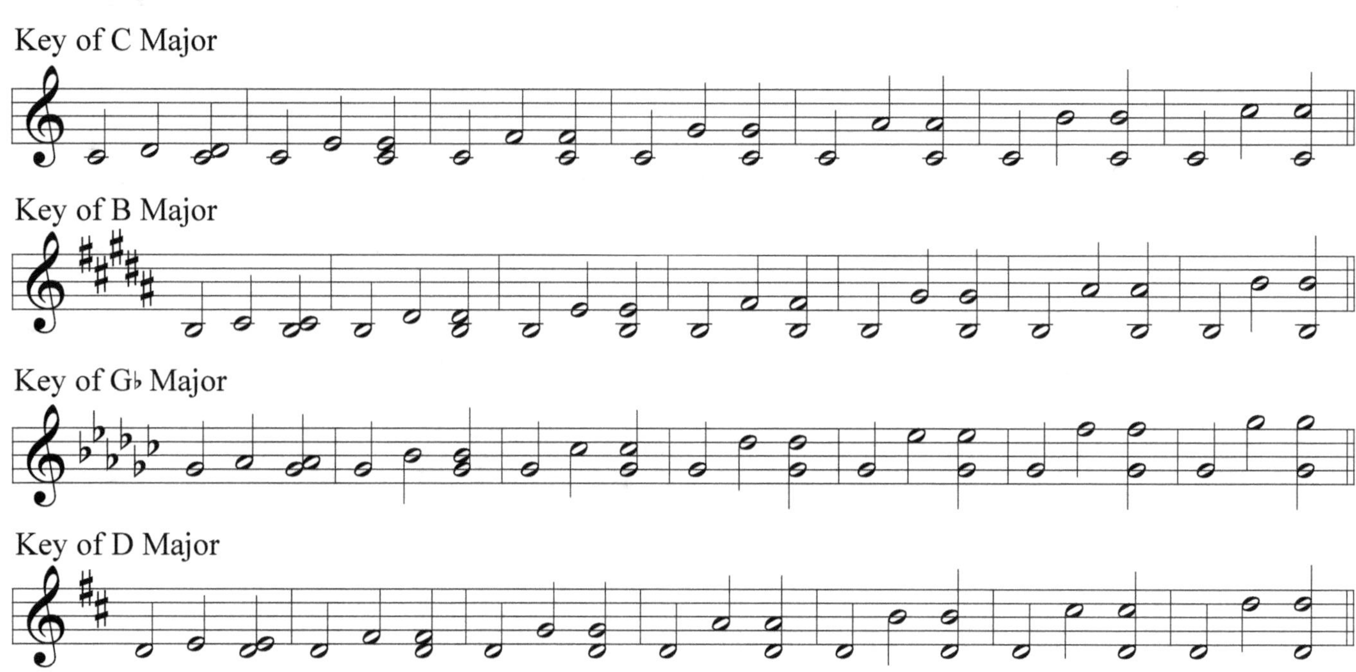

On the piano keyboard below, you can see the distance between the intervals. If you have a piano, keyboard, or piano app, play and sing these notes so you can hear the difference between the intervals.

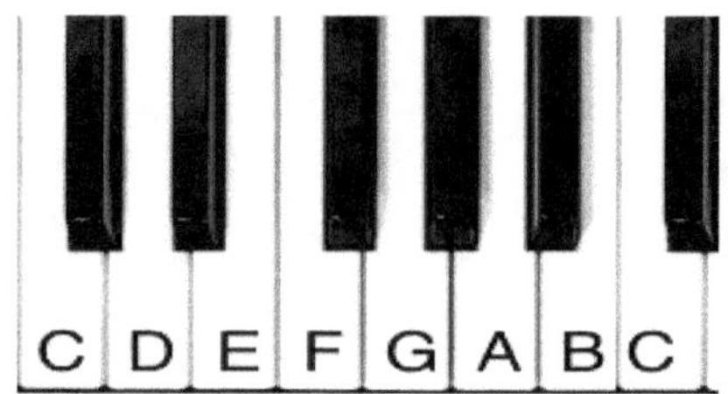

C-D is a 2nd   C-E is a 3rd   C-F is a 4th   C-G is a 5th   C-A is a 6th   C-B is a 7th   C-C is an octave

Review: Lesson 5

1. Circle all of the harmonic octaves (8ths).

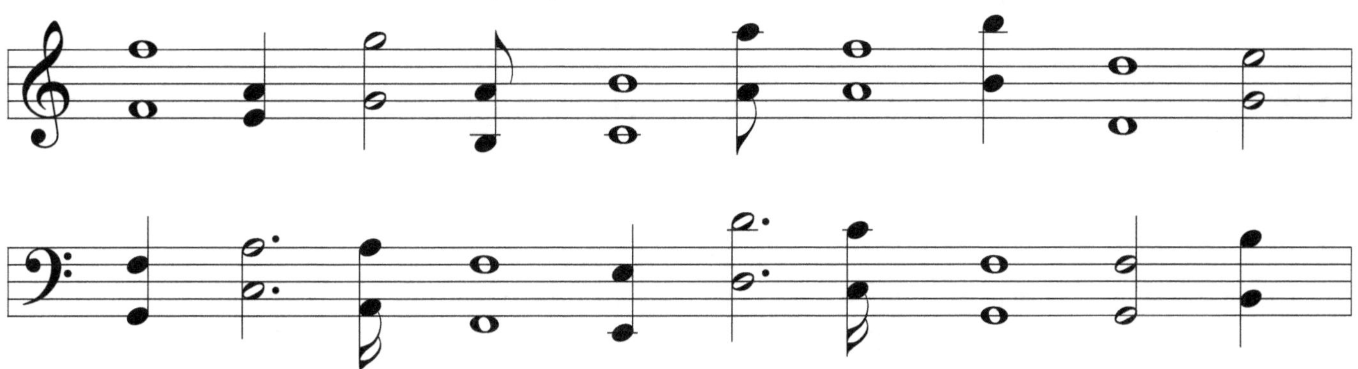

2. Label each melodic interval as a 2nd, 3rd, 4th, 5th, 6th, 7th, or 8th (octave).

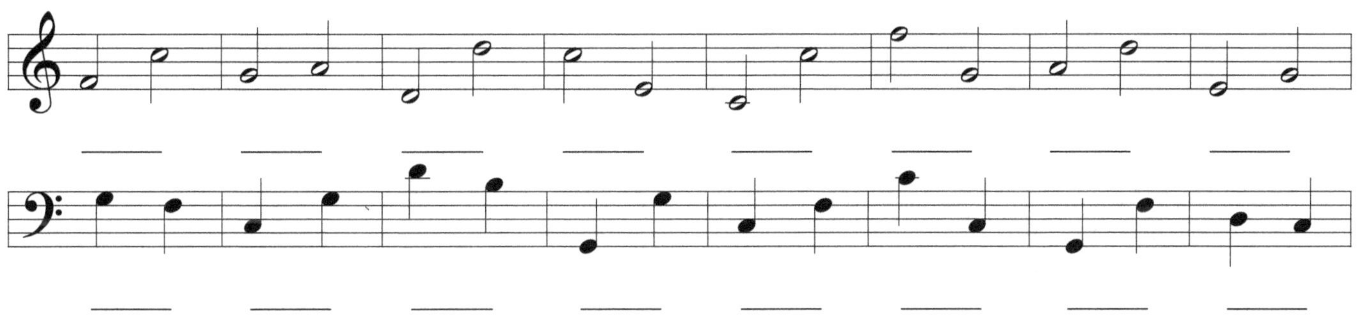

3. Name each interval: 2nd, 3rd, 4th, 5th, 6th, 7th, or 8th (octave).

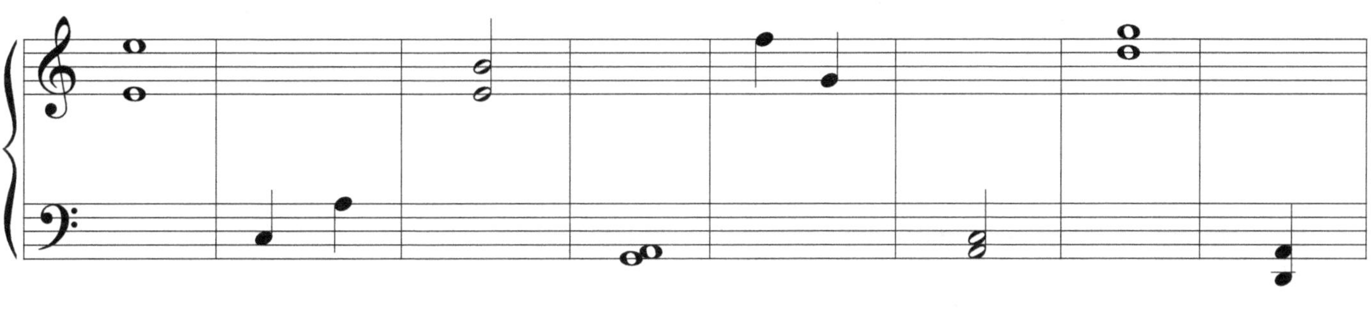

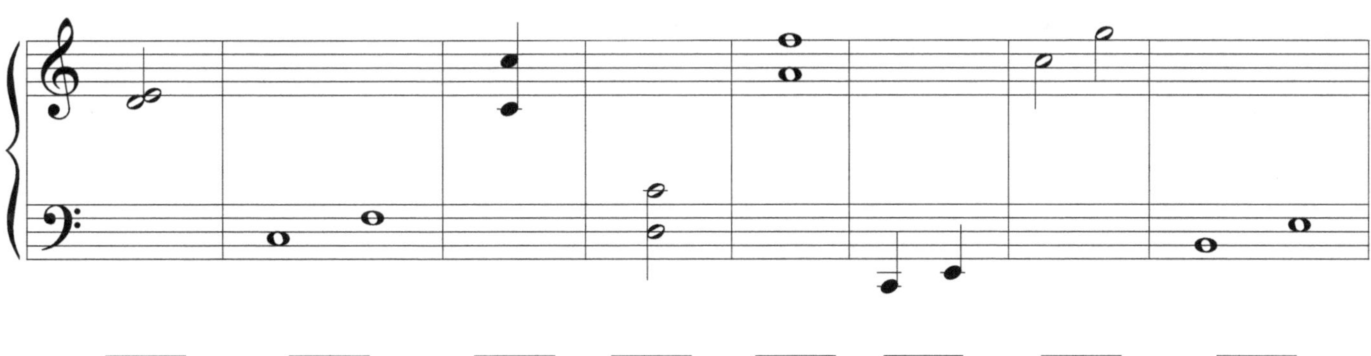

4. Add one note per measure to complete the requested melodic intervals.
Add the note after and above the given note. Make sure you add stems in the correct direction.
Use half notes. The first one is done for you.

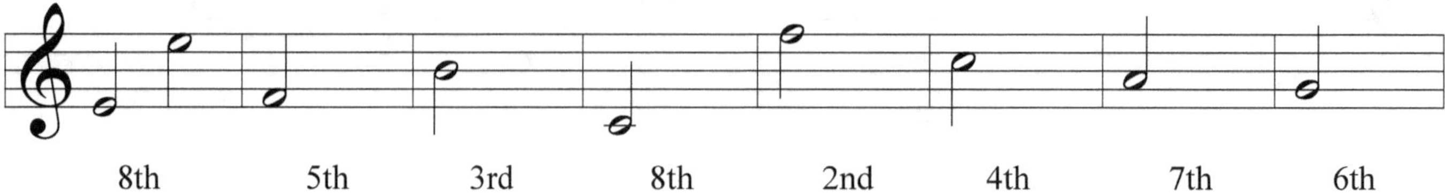

5. Add one note per measure to complete the requested melodic intervals.
Add the note after and below the given note. Make sure you add stems in the correct direction.
Use quarter notes. The first one is done for you.

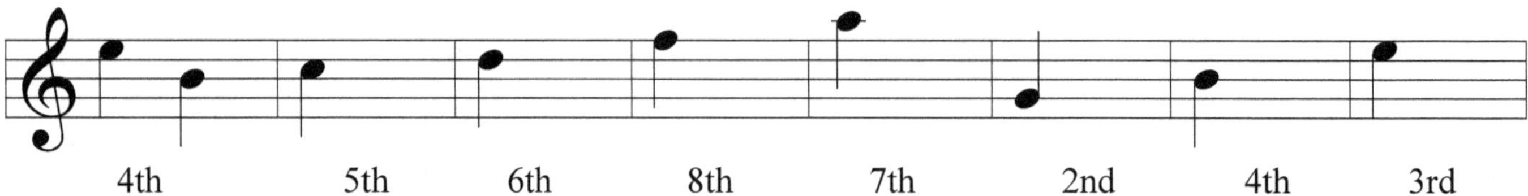

6. Add one note per measure to complete the requested harmonic intervals.
Add the note above the given note.
Use whole notes. The first one is done for you.

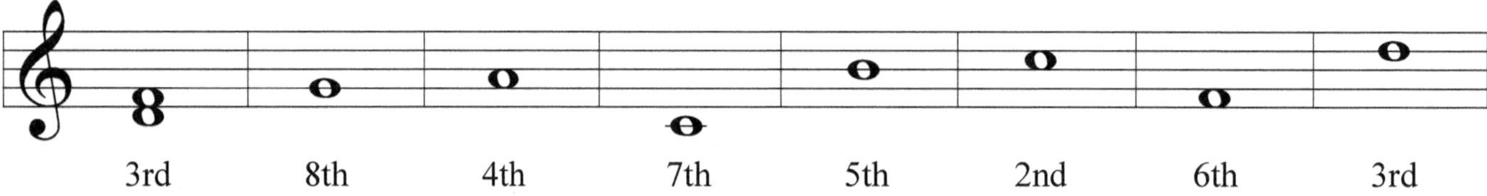

7. Add one note per measure to complete the requested harmonic intervals.
Add the note below the given note.
Use whole notes. The first one is done for you.

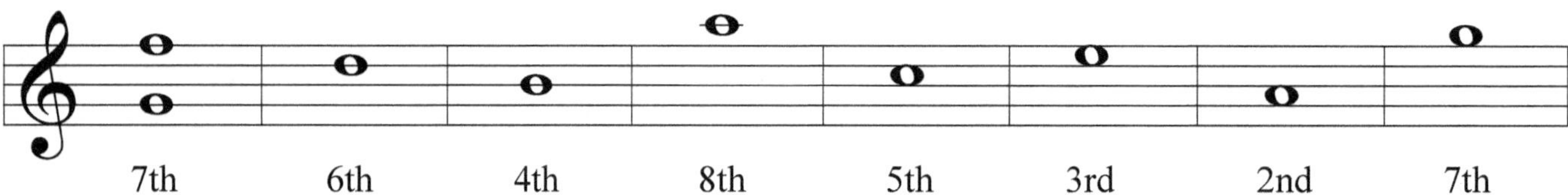

Lesson 6: Vocal Diction & IPA, Italian/Latin Diction

Every time we sing a song, we are telling a story. As singers, we have to be exceptionally clear with how we pronounce the words of our songs, or our audience will not understand us and our story will not be told.

If you reference a dictionary in any Latin based language (English, Italian, French, German, Spanish, Latin, etc.) you will see some symbols next to the words. These symbols make up the International Phonetic Alphabet, or IPA. The IPA represents the sounds of a language. In fact, the IPA represents nearly any vowel or consonant made by human beings!

In this lesson, we'll focus on a few of the sounds in the IPA. You will learn what the letter looks like in our language, what the IPA symbol for that letter is, and what it sounds like. The IPA symbols from Level 1-3 will also be in a chart on the following page.

Before we look at the symbols, make a couple of sounds so you can see all of the different positions your tongue moves to in order to make each sound.

Say "ah" as in the word "father," and "ee" as in the word "meet." You'll notice that when you say "ah," your tongue is at the bottom of your mouth, and when you say "ee" the center of your tongue moves to the roof of your mouth, while the tip remains down and behind the bottom teeth. When singing, we must be aware of any tension in our tongue, and ensure that it is in the proper position for creating accurate vowel sounds.

Here is a chart of the vowels we will learn in this lesson, along with their english equivalent.

oʊ (diphthong: 2 vowel sounds)	goat	[goʊt]	Low tongue, tip behind bottom teeth Lips open then rounded
aɪ (diphthong: 2 vowel sounds)	price	[praɪs]	Low tongue then high tongue tip behind bottom teeth then sides touching top teeth Lips tall then relaxed
ʤ	jar	[ʤɑr]	High tongue on hard palate tip behind top teeth Lips rounded
j	yet	[jɛt]	High tongue sides touching top teeth tip behind bottom teeth Lips relaxed
ʃ	ship	[ʃɪp]	High tongue sides touching top teeth Lips rounded

Courtesy of Sarah Sandvig

Practice saying the sounds above, and the english words in the second column.

Check that your tongue and lips are in the position described in the last column.

Additional IPA symbols, like the ones you see in the 3rd column will be introduced in later levels of these books.

Below is a chart of the vowels introduced in Levels 1, 2 & 3, followed by the new IPA symbols for this level.

Practice looking at each symbol, then say the english word and pay attention to the tongue and lips position described in the third column.

IPA SYMBOL	SOUND IN ENGLISH WORD	IPA SPELLING OF WORD	TONGUE/LIPS PLACEMENT
i	ski	[ski]	Center of tongue is high Lips relaxed
ɛ	led	[lɛd]	Low tongue Lips relaxed
ɑ	father	[ˈfɑðər]	Low tongue Lips relaxed
o	obey	[oʊˈbeɪ]	Low tongue, tip behind bottom teeth Rounded lips
u	goose	[gus]	Low tongue, tip behind bottom teeth Rounded lips
ɪ	kit	[kit]	High tongue, sides touching top teeth Lips relaxed
e	egg (first vowel sound you hear)	[feɪs]	High tongue, sides touching top teeth Lips relaxed
ə	afraid	[əˈfreɪd]	Mid tongue, tip behind bottom teeth Lips relaxed
æ	cat	[kæt]	Mid tongue, tip behind bottom teeth Lips slightly horizontal
ʊ	book	[bʊk]	Low tongue, tip below bottom teeth Lips relaxed
ʌ	strut	[strʌt]	Low tongue, tip behind bottom teeth Lips relaxed
ɔ	forest	[fɔrəst]	Low tongue, tip behind bottom teeth Lips slightly rounded
oʊ (diphthong: 2 vowel sounds)	goat	[goʊt]	Low tongue, tip behind bottom teeth Lips open then rounded
aɪ (diphthong: 2 vowel sounds)	price	[praɪs]	Low tongue then high tongue tip behind bottom teeth then sides touching top teeth Lips tall then relaxed
ʤ	jar	[ʤɑr]	High tongue on hard palate tip behind top teeth Lips rounded
j	yet	[jɛt]	High tongue sides touching top teeth tip behind bottom teeth Lips relaxed
ʃ	ship	[ʃɪp]	High tongue sides touching top teeth Lips rounded

Courtesy of Sarah Sandvig

Italian/Latin Diction

When you first learn a song in a foreign language, Italian and Latin are two of the easier languages to pronounce. Below are some rules for speaking/singing words in Italian and Latin that can help you learn how to prounounce the text in your songs.

It's also a great idea to use a translation app or website to hear someone pronounce the foreign language text as well.

As with any language, practicing speaking this language with an Italian accent will help with pronunciation. IPA is included in parentheses after each Italian/Latin word.

Remember: No diphthongs!
•*Core* (kore) is pronounced Core-A, but without the E sound at the end of A.
Another example is *Mio* (m'io) is pronounced Mee-oh but without the oo sound and the end of O.

•I's are pronounced like E's. (ie) *Ma'mi* (mami) is pronounced Mamee

•All R's are rolled or flipped. If you cannot roll your R's, try something similar to a D. *Caro* (karo) would sound similar to *Cah-doh*, then add a little less pressure to the roof of your mouth. Your tongue touches the top of your hard palate behind your top front teeth for the first letter.
**Two great practice exercises to learn how to roll your tongue is to say "Podda tea" over and over again, or try saying"Tah-dah" over and over again.

•A "C" followed by an E or I is pronounced as a "CH." (ie) *Facil* (fatʃil) is pronounced Facheel.
Also *Dolce* (doltʃe) is pronounced Dole-cheh.
•A "CH" combo is pronounced as a K. (ie) *Chiaro* (kjaro) is pronounced Kee-ah-ro.

•When a word has a double consonant, you stop on the first consonant then continue. The best example of this is the word "*Pizza*" (piddza). It's not pronounced PEEZA, it's pronounced PEETSA.
Also *Quella* (kwella) is Kwell-lah.

•A "G" if it's before an e or an i is a soft g. (ie) *gentil* (dʒentil) is pronounced jenteel, *Giardi* (dʒardi) is pronounced Jar-dee.
•A "G" followed by an "L" is silent. (ie) *scegliera* (ʃeʎʎera) is pronounced shay-lee-err-ah.
•A G followed by an H is pronounced as a Hard G...*Lunghezza* (luŋgettsa) is pronounced Loon-get-tsa.

•*Que* (kwe) is pronounced Kway.
•*Che* (ke) is pronounced Kay.

•An S followed by a C is pronounced as an SH. (ie) *s'angoscia* (ssaŋgoʃʃa) is zan-go-shee-ah.
•If an S is followed by a CH it's pronounced as SK. (ie) *scherzosa* (skertsoza) is scare-tso-za.
•A single S between two vowels is pronounced as a Z. (ie) *ascosa* (askoza) is pronounced ah-sko-za.
•An SC before e or i is pronounced as an SH. (ie) *scegliera* (ʃeʎʎera) is pronounced shay-lee-err-ah.

•An H at the beginning of a word is silent. (ie) *Hanno* (anno) is pronounced Ahn-no.

•A Z is pronounced like TS. (ie) *Danza* (dantsa) is pronounced Dawn-tsa.

•An "A" is pronounced as an "AH"

Review: Lesson 6

1. Check the English word that contains the same sound as the given IPA symbol.

aɪ	___Mice ___Bit	ʌ	___Nut ___Late	e	___Lay ___Met	j	___Jack ___Yes
oʊ	___Foot ___Boat	ʊ	___Look ___Luck	ɪ	___Might ___Pit	ɛ	___Meet ___Red
a	___Bite ___Bat	æ	___Bait ___Bat	u	___Loose ___But	i	___Bee ___Right
ɔ	___North ___Booth	ə	___Allow ___Egg	ʃ	___Short ___Send	ʤ	___Joy ___Drown

2. Circle the correct answer for the proper tongue and lip position for each IPA symbol. Say each sound, it will help!

i - Tongue is - high - and lips are - relaxed -
- low - - rounded -

a - Tongue is - mid - and lips are - tall & relaxed -
- low - - rounded -

æ - Tongue is - mid - and lips are - horizontal -
- low - - vertical -

j - Tongue is - mid - and lips are - relaxed -
- high - - rounded -

3. Write a word in the blank provided that uses the given IPA sound. Don't use any of the words from above or on the previous pages!

aɪ ______________	ʌ ______________	e ______________
oʊ ______________	ʊ ______________	ɪ ______________
a ______________	æ ______________	u ______________
ɔ ______________	ə ______________	o ______________
ɑ ______________	ɛ ______________	i ______________
ʤ ______________	ʃ ______________	j ______________

4. Circle "True" or "False" for the following questions about Italian and Latin pronunciation.

When you have two of the same consonants in a row, you pause after the first one, as in "pizza."

True False

All R's are pronounced with a curled tongue as they are in American English.

True False

All S's are pronounced like a Z.

True False

5. For the following questions, check the correct choice that best describes how the Italian/Latin word would be pronounced.

Che ___Keh
___Chay

Que ___Keh
___Kweh

Scherza ___Share-zah
___Scare-tsa

Dolce ___Dole-cheh
___Dole-say

Bella ___Bell-la
___Bell-lay

Tutto ___Tut-toe
___Toot-toe

Voi ___Vo-ee
___Vo-eye

Mio ___Mee-oh
___My-oh

Pietà ___Pie-tah
___Pee-yea-tah

Verum ___Veh-room
___Vee-rum

Chiaro ___Key-ah-roh
___Chee-ah-roh

Sai ___Saw-ee
___Say-ee

Mezzo ___Met-tso
___Mezo

Amore ___Eh-more
___Ah-more-eh

Così ___Cozay
___Ko-zee

Dura ___Doo-rah
___Duh-rah

Ave ___Eh-va
___Ah-veh

Domine ___Doh-my-nee
___Dom-mee-neh

Opera ___Oh-pair-ah
___Opp-pair-ah

Gentile ___Shh-en-tee-leh
___Jen-tee-lay

Lesson 7: Sight-Singing

In order to learn a song, singers learn to read both rhythmic patterns and notes (melody) on the staff. Singing a melody for the first time is called "sight-singing." Below are some rhythmic examples using the notes introduced so far.

Hint: When singing rhythmic examples, take a breath on the rests: then you won't miss them! *Tap* and *say* the beats, then sing the examples on La (choose any pitch that suits your voice).

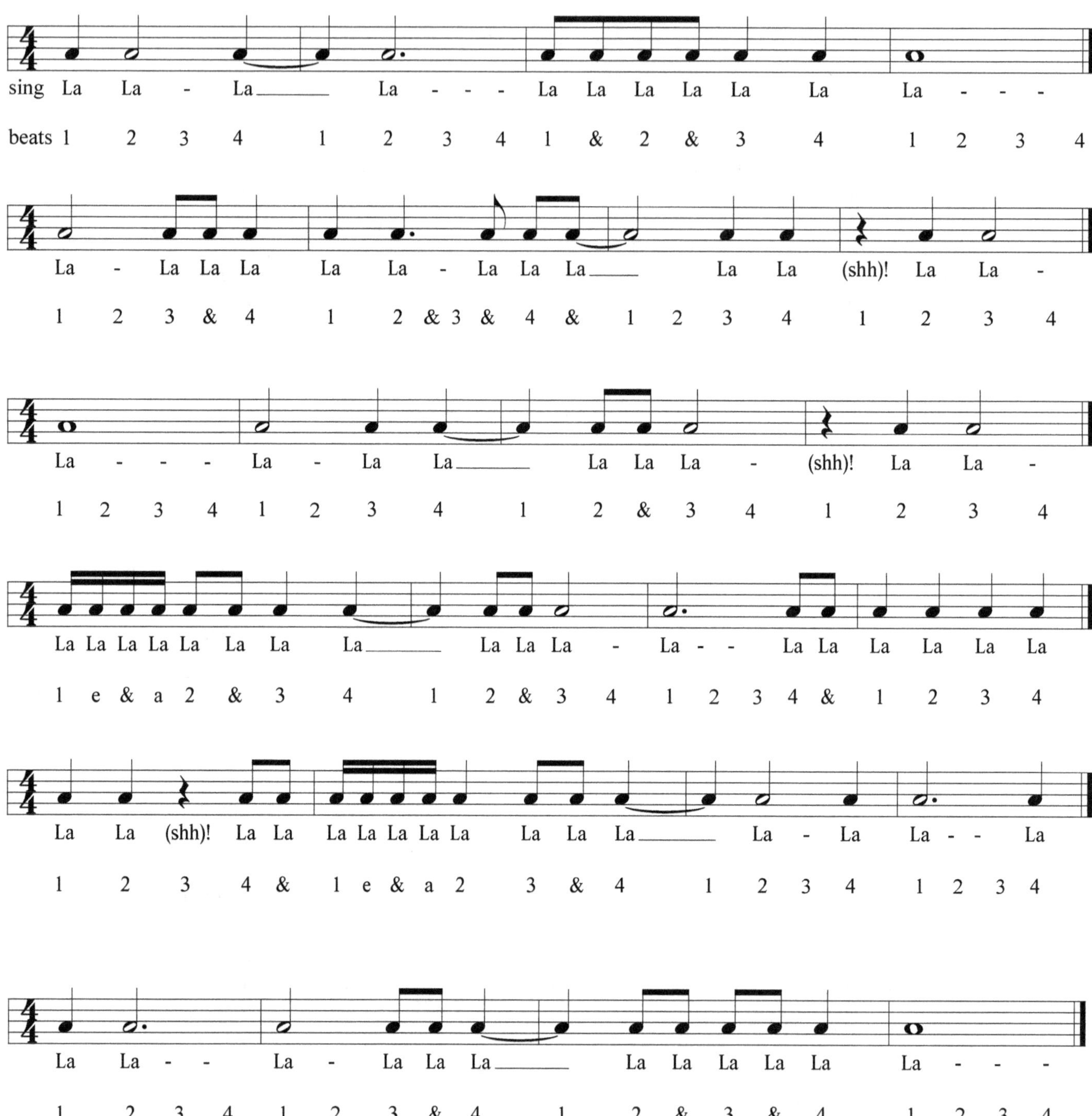

Melody & Solfege

Solfege is a system of assigning a syllable to each note of a scale, just like in the song "Do-Re-Mi" from the musical *The Sound of Music.*

Solfege is a useful tool when sight-singing. Moveable "Do" is when "Do" matches the **root** of whatever key you're in. The following examples contain Major scales from the new keys covered in this level.

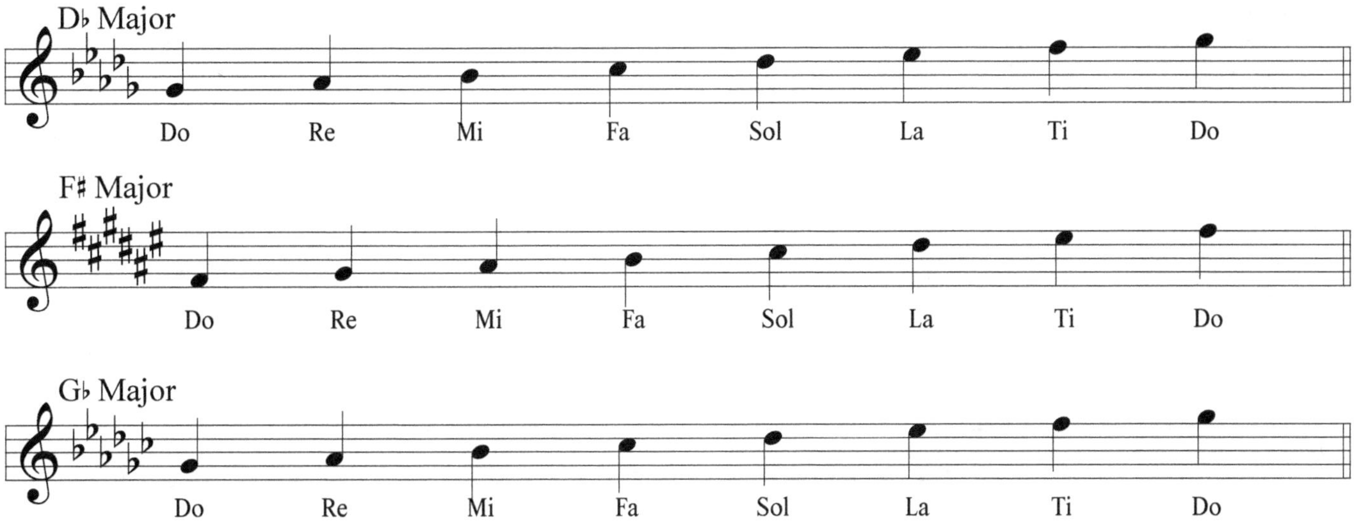

In this Level, you'll learn to sing melodies with Do, Re, Mi, Fa, Sol & La. The following melodies have the solfege written under the notes for you. Pay attention to the key signature changes. Use the picture of the piano below to find your starting note on your piano or piano app.

Here are some examples in F & G Major (high voices), and D & C Major (lower voices).

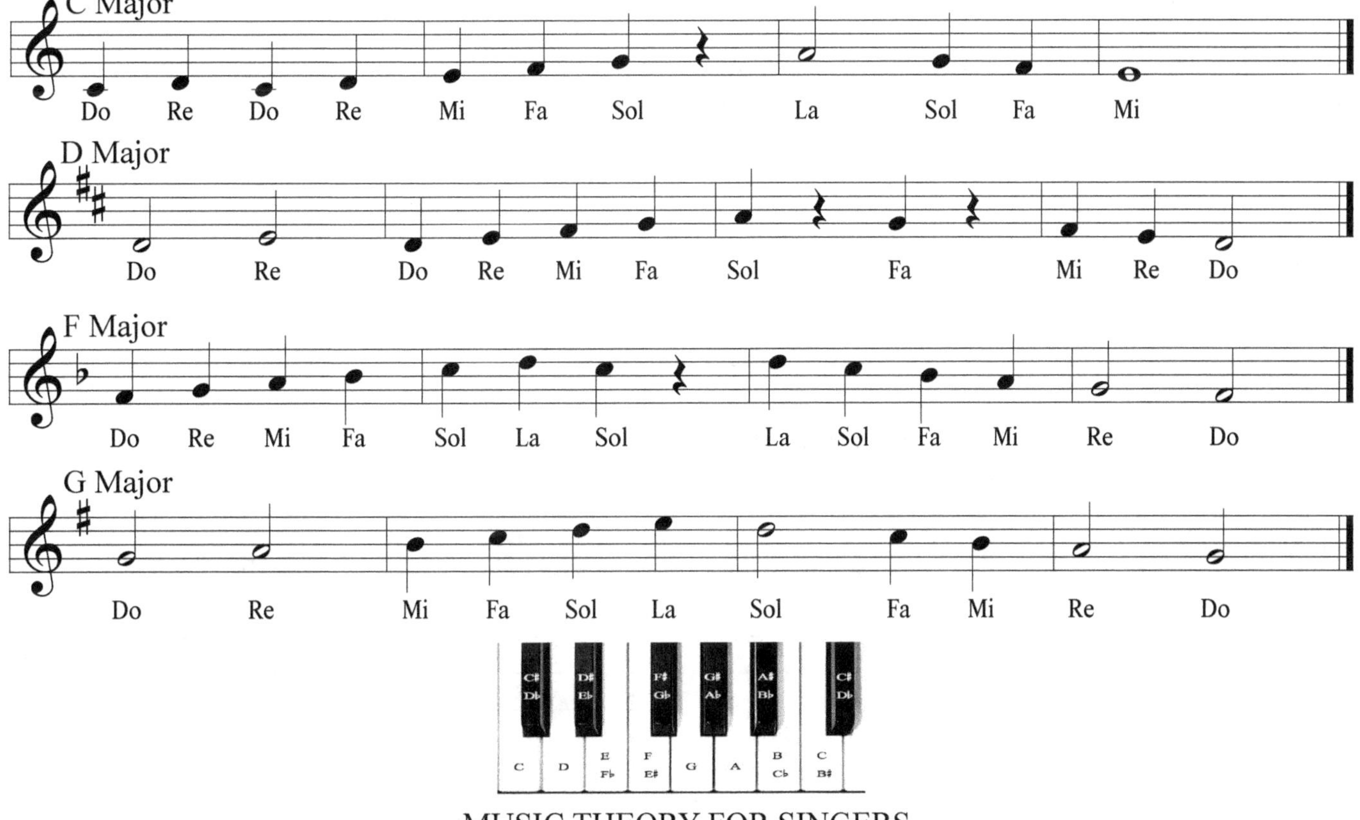

Review: Lesson 7

1. For the following melodies, write the note names, solfege & beats underneath the notes. Practice singing the examples when you are done!

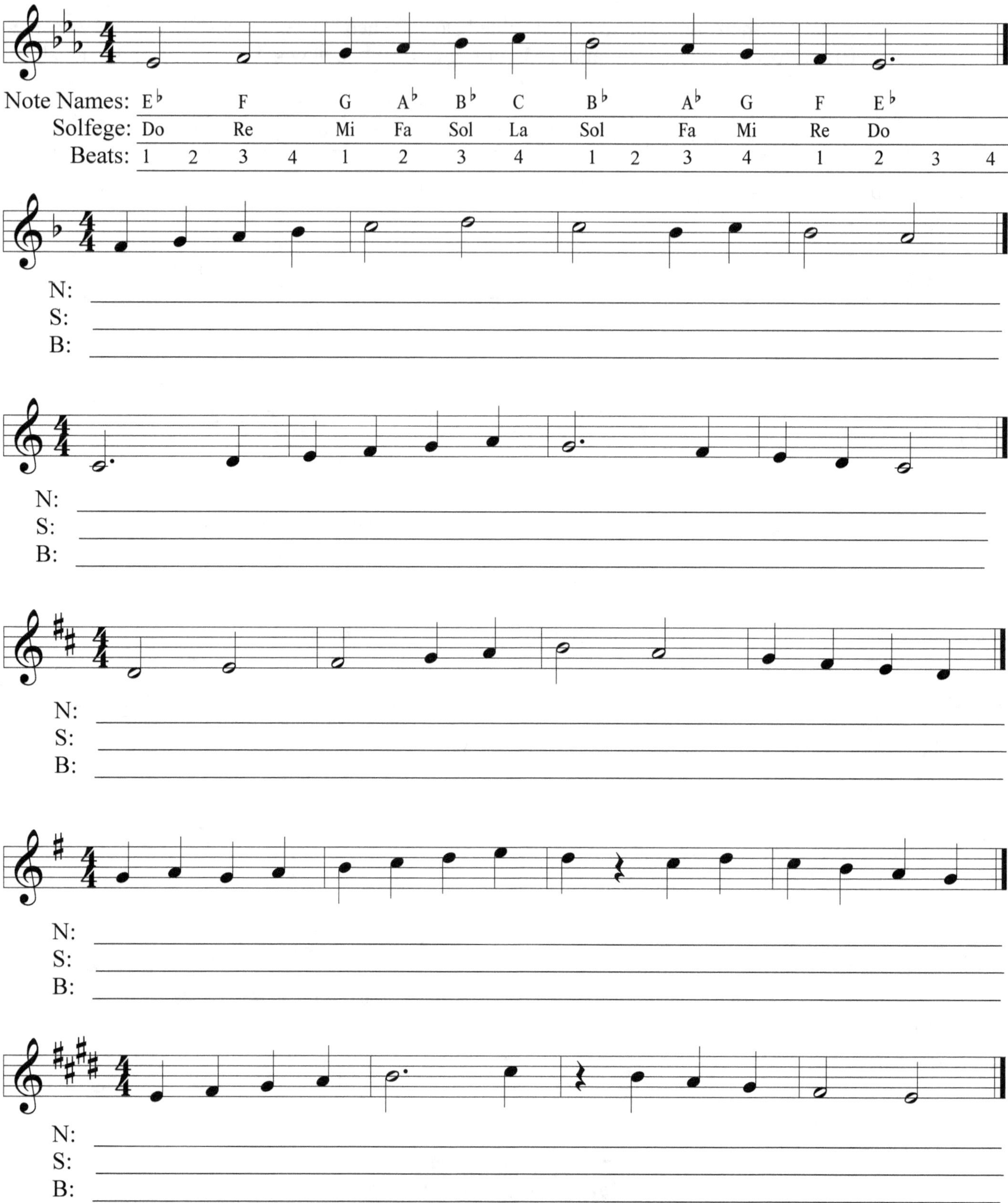

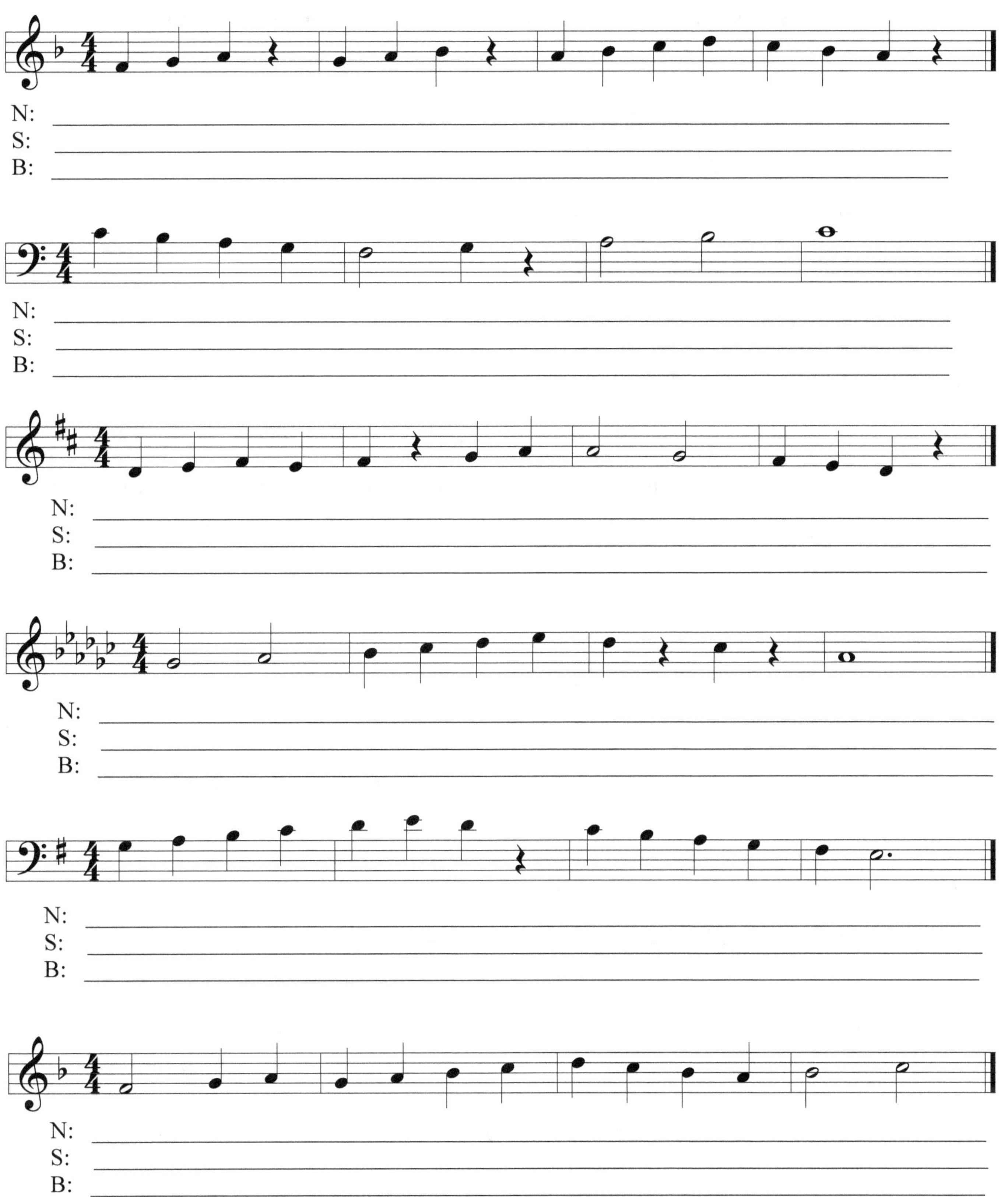
N:
S:
B:
N:
S:
B:
N:
S:
B:
N:
S:
B:
N:
S:
B:
N:
S:
B:

Lesson 8: Musical Terms

A crucial part of understanding music is being able to recognize and define musical terms. Below is a list of terms covered in this level.

accelerando (accel.)- becoming faster

adagio- a slow tempo falling between largo (slower) and andante (faster)

allegretto- a light, cheerful tempo, a bit slower than allegro

andantino- a little faster tempo than andante

con moto- with motion

diphthong- a vowel with two sounds

half step- the smallest musical interval between two adjacent notes in a 12-tone scale, e.g. Mi-Fa

IPA- the International Phonetic Alphabet: a standard representation of the sounds of spoken language

Jazz music- began in America around 1900, influenced by African & European traditions. It incorporates blues, ragtime, swing, improvisation, syncopation & complex rhythms.

larghetto- a slow tempo, a little faster than largo

largo- slow and broad

meno mosso- less lively, slower

opera- a play in which the characters sing rather than speak, accompanied by instruments

più mosso- more lively, faster

rallentando (rall.)- becoming gradually slower

Romantic period of music- a 19th Century movement in the arts that influenced music from about 1800 until 1920

sempre- always

senza- without

whole step- the interval of a major 2nd; consists of 2 half steps, e.g. Do-Re

Review: Lesson 8

1. Check the appropriate answer for each of the following questions.

a. The Italian term *Sempre* means:

____without

____always

b. A half step is the same as:

____"Do-Re"

____"Mi-Fa"

c. A vowel with two sounds is called a:

____diphthong

____schwa

d. *Accelerando* means to become:

____gradually faster

____gradually slower

e. This Italian term means "less lively."

____più mosso

____meno mosso

f. The Italian term *con moto* means:

____with motion

____with feeling

g. This period of music was between 1820-1920.

____Romantic Period

____Classical Period

h. The Italian term *largo* means:

____quick, lively

____slow and broad

i. The tempo *Andantino* is:

____a little faster than Andante

____a little slower than Andante

j. The tempo *Allegretto* is:

____a little slower than Allegro

____a little faster than Allegro

2. Complete the following crossword puzzle using the terms from this level.

Level 4 Crossword

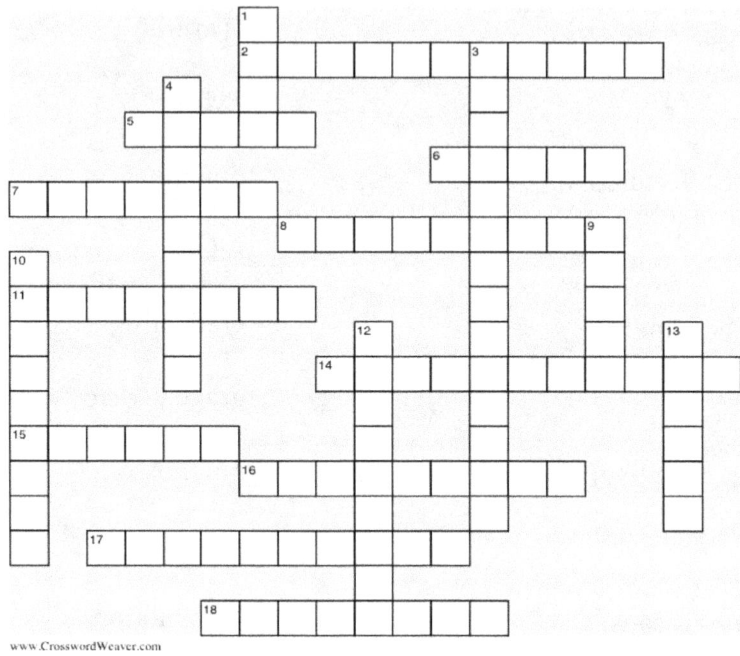

ACROSS

2 becoming faster
5 without
6 slow and broad
7 with motion (two words)
8 a little faster tempo than andante
11 the smallest musical interval between two adjacent notes in a 12-tone scale (two words)
14 becoming gradually slower
15 always
16 a vowel with two sounds
17 a light, cheerful tempo, a bit slower than allegro
18 more lively, faster (two words)

DOWN

1 form of music that began in America around 1900, influenced by African & European traditions. It incorporates blues, ragtime, swing, improvisation, syncopation & complex rhythms.
3 a 19th Century movement in the arts that influenced music from 1820 until 1920 (two words)
4 less lively, slower (two words)
9 a play in which the characters sing rather than speak, accompanied by instruments
10 the interval of a major 2nd; consists of 2 half steps (two words)
12 a slow tempo, a little faster than largo
13 a slow tempo falling between largo (slower) and andante (faster)

crossword created at:
www.CrosswordWeaver.com

Lesson 9: Spotlight on Composers

An important part of music education is learning about the history of music. Studying composers allows for understanding the music we sing and why it was written the way it was. In this level you will learn about Wolfgang Amadeus Mozart and Felix Mendelssohn.

WOLFGANG AMADEUS MOZART

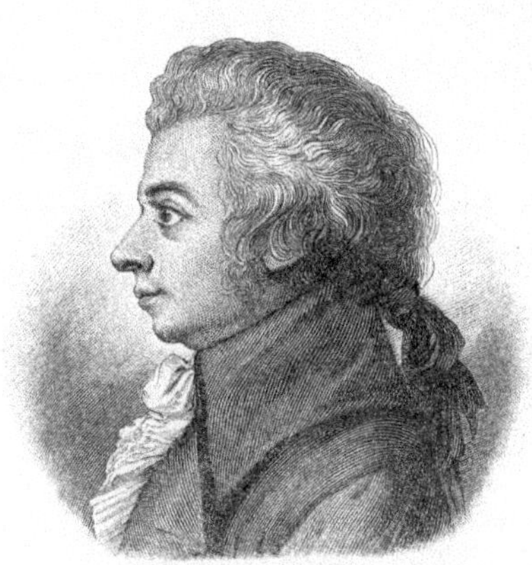

Wolfgang Amadeus Mozart was born in the Classical period of music on January 27, 1756 in Salzburg, Austria. His father began to teach him piano when he was four years old, and he was already composing pieces by the age of five. Mozart's father, Leopold, took his family on several European tours, showing off his incredibly talented children, Wolfgang and his sister Nannerl. Leopold took Mozart on a tour to Italy beginning in 1769. Mozart wrote his first opera, *Mitridate, re di ponto* which was a success. He wrote more operas and the famous motet *Exsultate, jubilate, K. 165,* all between 1769-1772.

Mozart became court musician in Salzburg for Prince-Archbishop Colloredo and composed symphonies, sonatas, and some operas, to name a few. In 1781, Mozart's opera *Idomeneo* premiered with some success. Soon thereafter, Mozart left his job in Salzburg and decided to move to Vienna to be an independent composer and performer. He quickly gained the reputation of the best keyboard player in Vienna. In 1782, Mozart married Constanze Weber. They had six children, only two of whom survived beyond infancy.

Mozart studied Johann Sebastian Bach and George Frederic Handel, who influenced his compositional style. Some of his "Baroque" elements can be heard in his opera *Die Zauberflöte* (The Magic Flute). In 1782, Mozart met Franz Joseph Haydn, and they became friends. Mozart also wrote several piano concertos and gave frequent concerts.

In 1785, Mozart began working with the librettist Lorenzo Da Ponte on the first of many opera they would write together, *The Marriage of Figaro*. Da Ponte also wrote the libretto for Mozart's operas *Don Giovanni* and *Cosi fan tutte.*

Mozart began to have some financial and health problems around 1786. During the last year of his life, however, he composerd some of his most well-known pieces. He wrote the opera *The Magic Flute* and his *Requiem* K. 626, which he was unable to finish before he died. Mozart died on December 5th, 1791 at the age of 35. The cause of death is unknown. Although he was buried in a common grave, there were several memorial services and concerts held in his honor.

Best Known Vocal Works:
23 Opera's including: ***Le Nozze di Figaro, Don Giovanni, Cosi Fan Tutte, Die Zauberflöte***
Hundreds of concert arias and songs including: **"Dans un Bois Solitaire," "Die Zauberer," "Das Veilchen," "Als Luise die Briefe ihres ungetreuen Liebhabers verbrannte," "Ridente la Calma," "An die Freude"**

Other Significant Works:
Hundreds of pieces for keyboard, string instruments, chamber groups and full symphony orchestras.
Film about Mozart: ***Amadeus*** (1984) - won over 40 awards, including 8 Academy Awards.

FELIX MENDELSSOHN

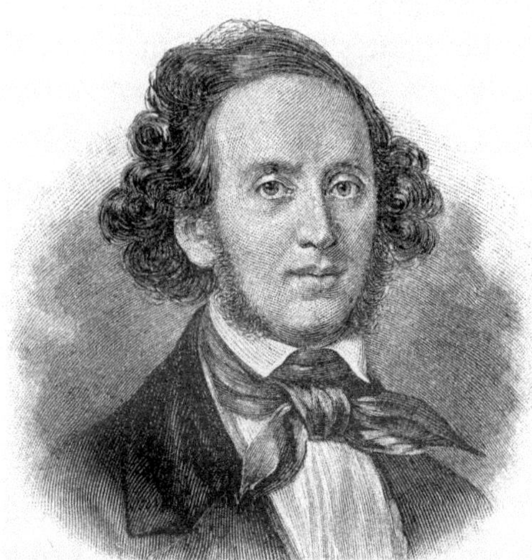
Felix Mendelssohn-Bartholdy.

Felix Mendelssohn was born in the Classical and early Romantic periods of music on February 3, 1809 in Hamburg, Germany. Like Mozart, Mendelssohn was thought of as a child prodigy. His mother started teaching him piano at age six. Then in 1819, he began studying with Carl Friedrich Zelter in Berlin. Mendelssohn gave his first public concert when he was nine years old.

By the time he was 15, Mendelssohn had written 12 string symphonies, a piano quartet (which was published), and his first sympohny for full orchestra (op. 11 in C minor). He wrote the *Wedding March* which is still used in nearly every wedding.

Mendelssohn's sister, *Fanny, grew up to be a well-known pianist and composer, but at the time it was not acceptable for women to have a career in music.

In 1821, Mendelssohn met the famous poet, Wolfgang von Goethe. He set several of Goethe's poems to music. He also made a name for himself conducting Bach's *St. Matthew Passion* in Berlin and Handel's *Israel in Egypt* in Düsseldorf. In 1835, Mendelssohn took the job of conductor of the Leipzig Gewandhaus Orchestra. It was here that he premiered his oratorio *St. Paul* after the death of his father.

In 1837, Felix married Cecile Charlotte Jeanrenaud. They had five children, four of whom survived into adulthood. Mendelssohn also had a relationship with the soprano Jenny Lind, for whom he wrote the unfinished opera *Lorelei.*

In 1843, Mendelssohn founded the Leipzig Conservatory. Some of the famous musicians who worked there with him were Robert Schumann and Joseph Joachim. Today, the conservatory is called the *Felix Mendelssohn Bartholdy University of Music and Theatre.*

Mendelssohn died on May 14, 1847 after a series of strokes. He was only 38 years old.

Best Known Vocal Works:
Art Songs including: **"Auf Flugeln des Gesanges" (On Wings of Song), "Neue Liebe"**
Choral Works including: ***St. Paul, Elijah, Christus*** (oratorios), ***Hark! The Herald Angels Sing*** (from his cantata ***Festgesang***)

*Some of Fanny's songs were also published under Felix's name.

Review: Lesson 9

1. Fill in the correct answer(s) to the following questions about Wolfgang Amadeus Mozart and Felix Mendelssohn.

Wolfgang Amadeus Mozart

a. Mozart was born in which country?______________________________

b. What musical period does he represent?________________________________

c. At what age did he begin composing music?_______________________________

d. Who is the famous librettist that Mozart collaborated with on his opera *The Marriage of Figaro* and *Don Giovanni*?_________________________________

e. What is the name of the unfinished piece he wrote the year of his death?______________________

f. How old was he when he died?________________________

Felix Mendelssohn

a. Mendelssohn was born in which country?_____________________________

b. Which musical periods does he represent?______________________and________________________

c. What was the name of his famous sister, who was also a pianist and composer?_________________

d. How old was he when he gave his first public concert?___________________

e. Mendelssohn met a famous poet in 1821 and set several of his poems to music. Name the poet.

________________________.

f. What is the name of the music school that he founded in 1843?__________________________________

Level 4 Review Test

Answer the questions about the following musical example. (13 points)

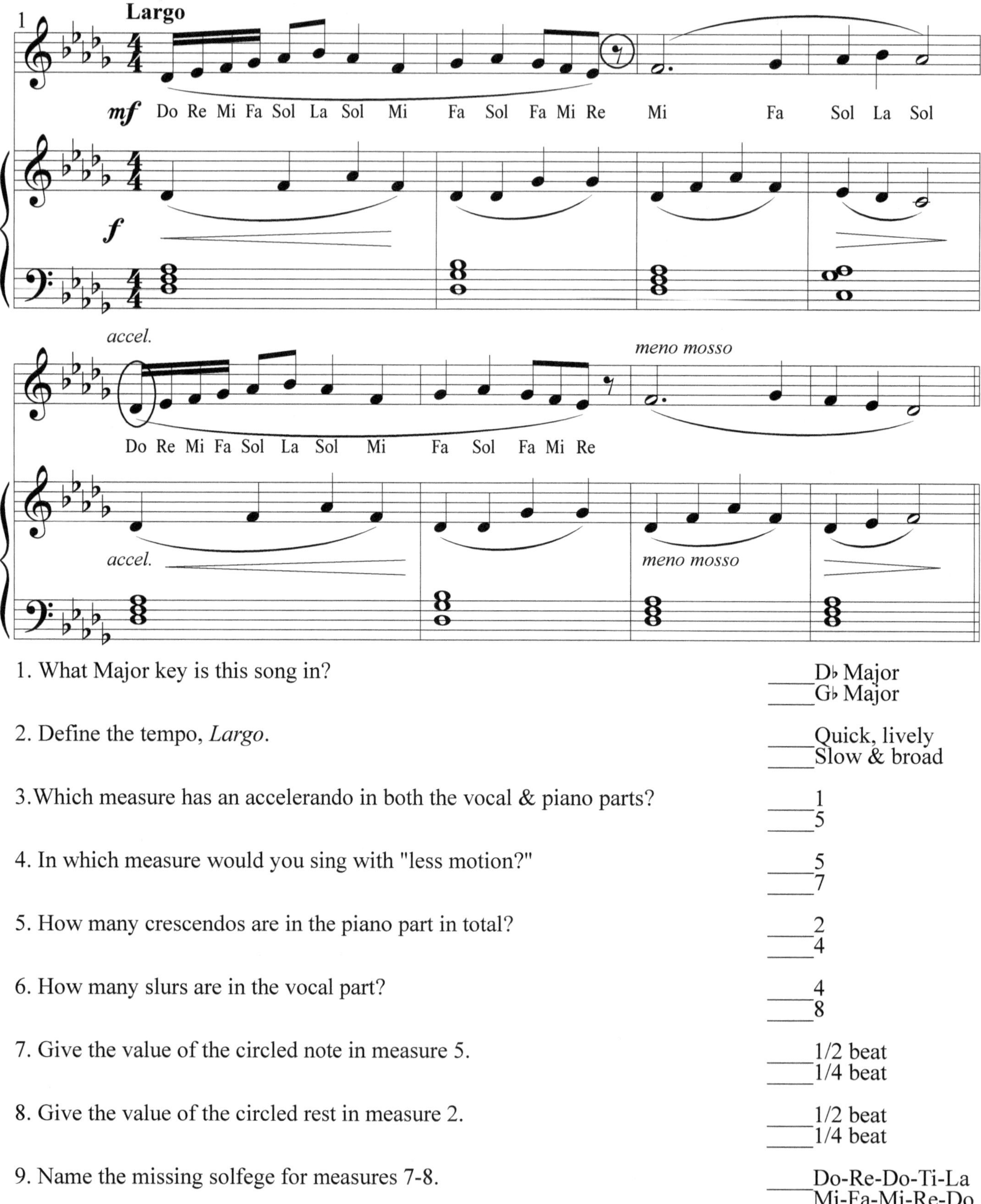

1. What Major key is this song in? ____D♭ Major ____G♭ Major

2. Define the tempo, *Largo*. ____Quick, lively ____Slow & broad

3. Which measure has an accelerando in both the vocal & piano parts? ____1 ____5

4. In which measure would you sing with "less motion?" ____5 ____7

5. How many crescendos are in the piano part in total? ____2 ____4

6. How many slurs are in the vocal part? ____4 ____8

7. Give the value of the circled note in measure 5. ____1/2 beat ____1/4 beat

8. Give the value of the circled rest in measure 2. ____1/2 beat ____1/4 beat

9. Name the missing solfege for measures 7-8. ____Do-Re-Do-Ti-La ____Mi-Fa-Mi-Re-Do

10. Name the following notes. (16 points)

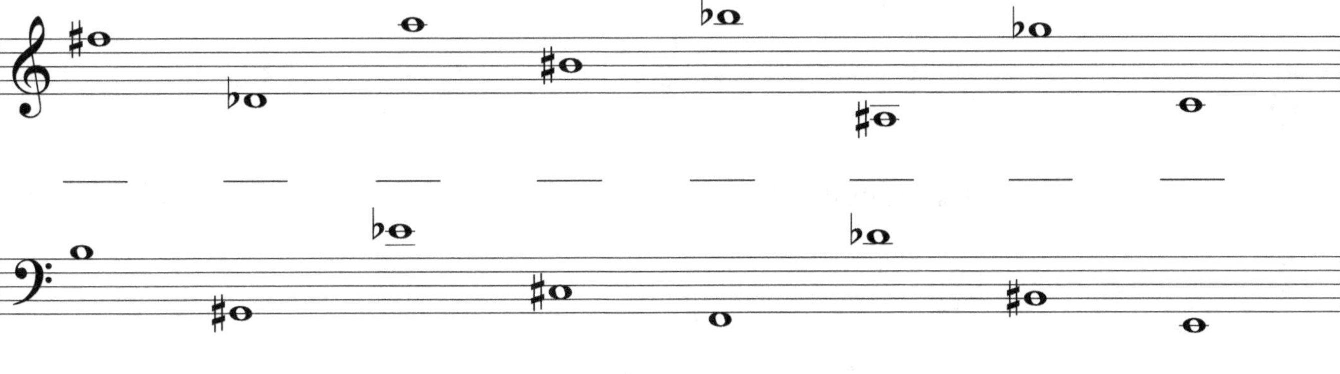

11. Name the following notes and their values *(for example: Half note, 2 beats).* (12 points)

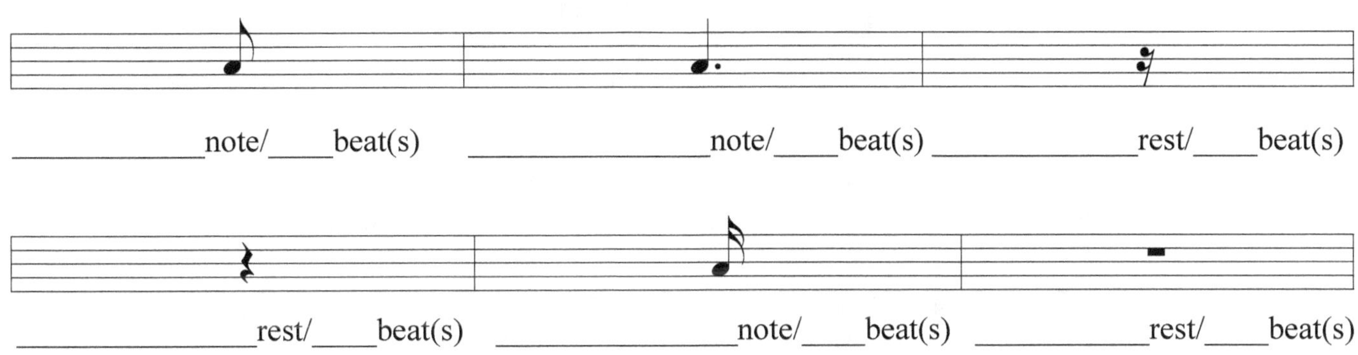

12. Add 3 bar lines and a double bar line to the following example. (4 points)

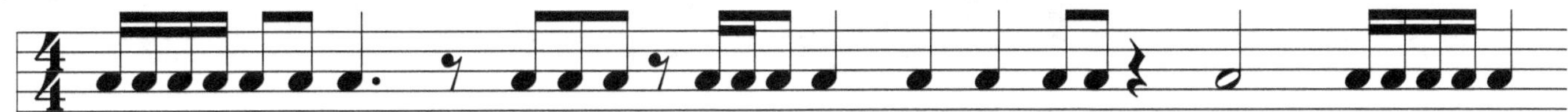

13. Add the missing time signature, then write the beats underneath the notes (5 points-one for time signature, one for each correct measure)

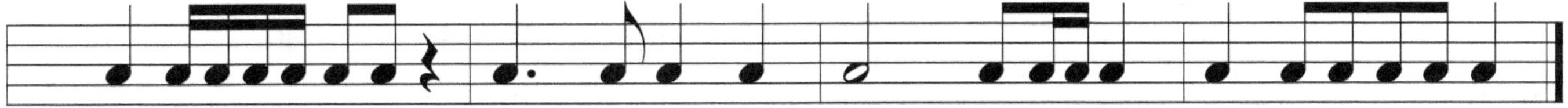

14. Name the key signature <u>and</u> interval for each example. (8 points)

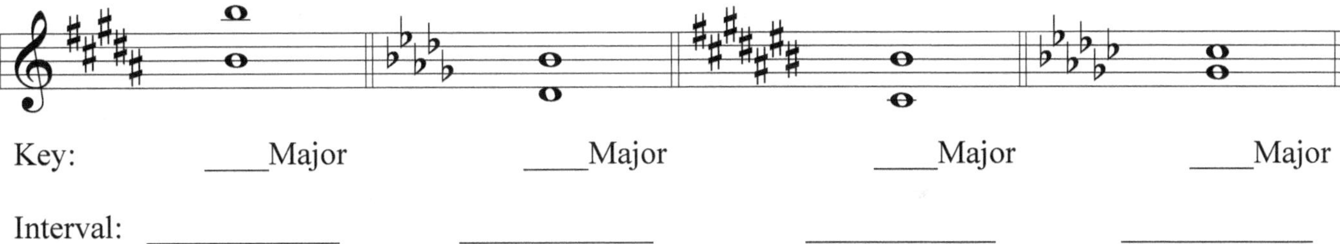

Key: ____Major ____Major ____Major ____Major

Interval: ____________ ____________ ____________ ____________

15. Draw the note a half step **higher** than the one given. Pay close attention to the key signatures. Use the keyboard below for help. (5 points)

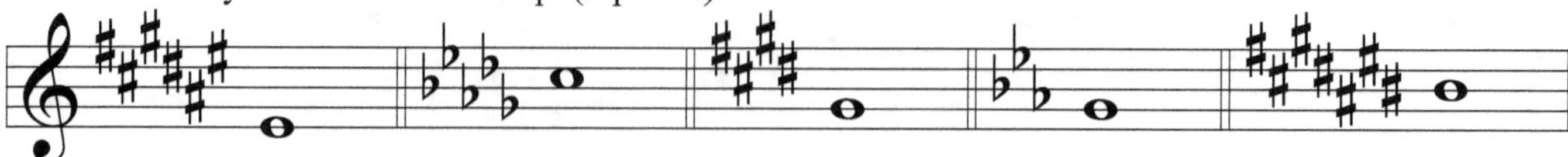

16. Draw the note a whole step **lower** than the one given. Use the keyboard below for help. (5 points)

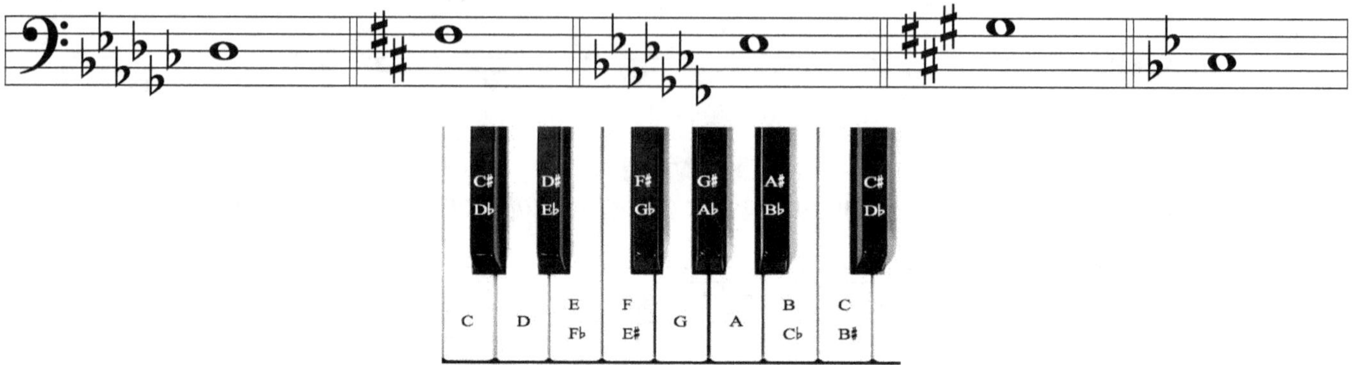

17. Each of these chords should have a Do (1), Mi (3), & Sol (5).
Fill in the missing note for each chord in both clefs to create a root position triad. (8 points)

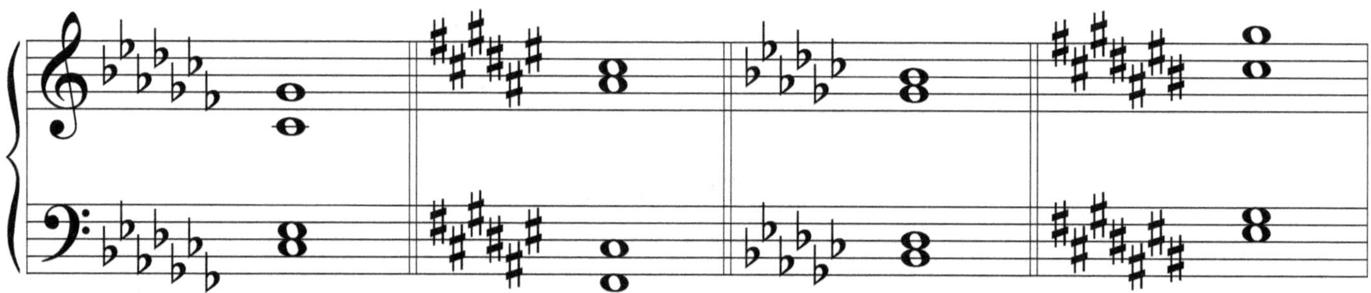

18. Draw a whole note above the given note to create the requested harmonic intervals. (8 points)

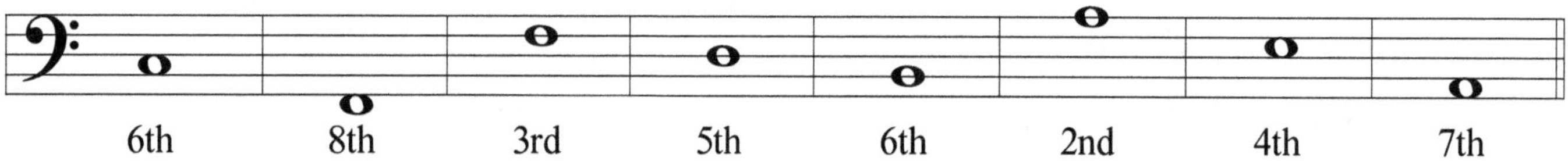

19. Write the note names and solfege directly under each note in the following examples. Don't forget to add ♯/♭ if needed. (8 points- 1 point per correct measure: both solfege and notes must be correct)

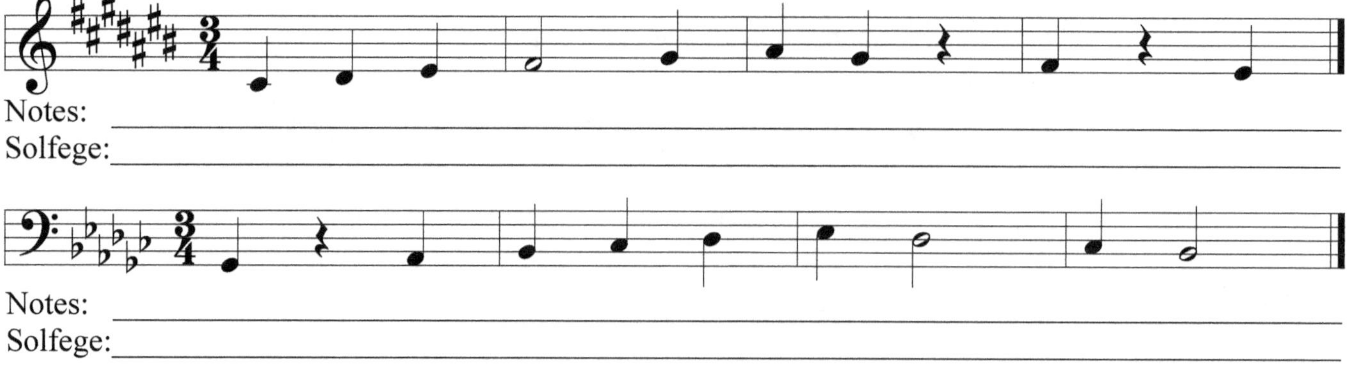

20. Check the English word that contains the same sound as the given IPA symbol. (8 points)

aɪ	____Nice ____Cake	ʤ	____Giraffe ____Dig	ʌ	____Beg ____Bug	j	____Blend ____Yes
oʊ	____Moat ____Ouch	ʃ	____Sound ____Shame	ʊ	____Crook ____Mug	ə	____Peg ____Alone

21. For the following questions, check the correct choice that best describes how the Italian/Latin word would be pronounced. The IPA spelling is provided for you, in parentheses, after the word. (4 points)

grazia (grat:tsja)	____graht-see-a ____great-a	chi (ki)	____chee ____key
terzetto (tertset:to)	____terzet-toh ____tare-tset-toh	deciso (detʃizo)	____date-cheese-oh ____det-shy-zo

22. Fill in the correct answer using the musical terms in this level. (5 points)

a. An____________________is a play in which the characters sing rather than speak, accompanied by instruments.

b. ____________________means "more lively, faster."

c. A____________________is the interval of a Major 2nd; consists of 2 half steps, e.g. Do-Re

d. A____________________is a vowel with two sounds.

e. ____________________is a little faster tempo than *andante.*

23. For the following questions about Mozart & Mendelssohn, write the correct word or composer in the space provided. (5 points)

a. ____________________was buried in a common grave.

b. Mendelssohn was __________ years old when he died.

c. Mozart toured Europe with his sister ____________________.

d. Mozart was friends with the composer Franz Joseph ____________________.

e. Mendelssohn wrote the famous Christmas carol ________________________________.

Final Score:____________/114

answer key begins on the next page

Level 4 Review Test: Answers

Answer the questions about the following musical example. (13 points)

1. What Major key is this song in? D♭ Major
2. Define the tempo, *Largo*. Slow & Broad
3. Which measure has an accelerando in both the vocal & piano parts? 5
4. In which measure whould you sing with "less motion?" 7
5. How many crescendos are in the piano part in total? 2
6. How many slurs are in the vocal part? 4
7. Give the value of the circled note in measure 5. 1/4 beat
8. Give the value of the circled rest in measure 2. 1/2 beat
9. Name the missing solfege for measures 7-8. Mi-Fa-Mi-Re-Do

10. Name the following notes. (16 points)

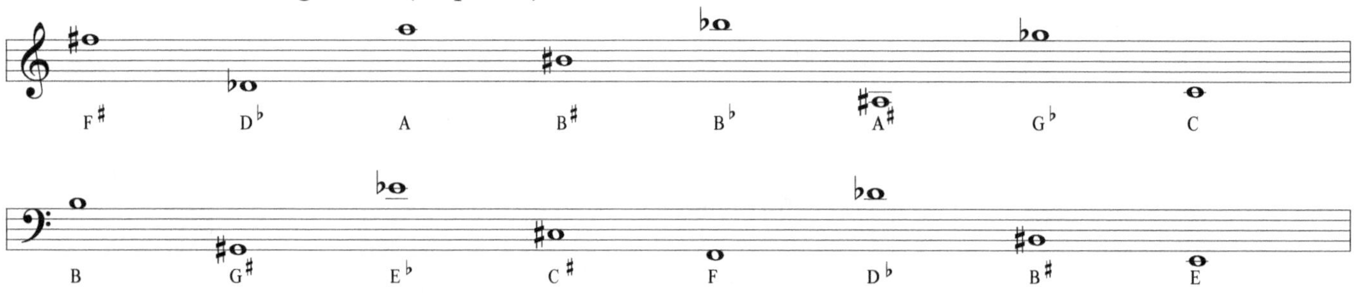

11. Name the following notes and their values *(for example: Half note, 2 beats)*. (12 points)

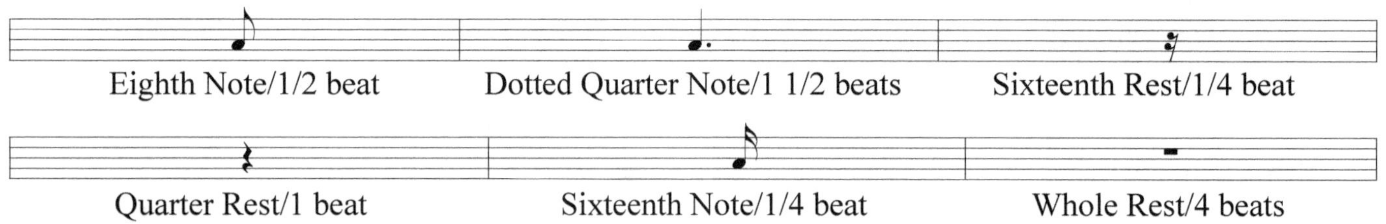

12. Add 3 bar lines and a double bar line to the following example. (4 points)

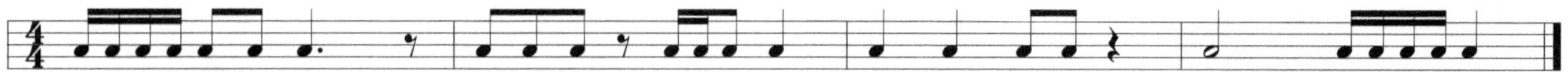

13. Add the missing time signature, then write the beats underneath the notes (5 points-one for time signature, one for each correct measure)

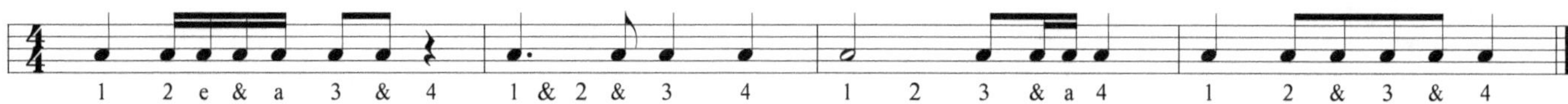

14. Name the key signature <u>and</u> interval for each example. (8 points)

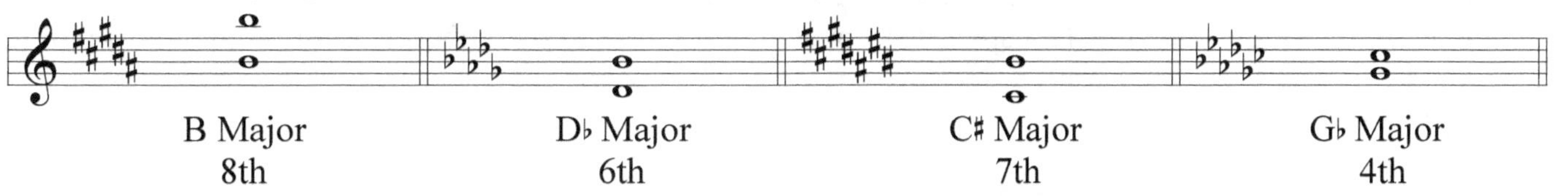

15. Draw the note a <u>half step</u> **<u>higher</u>** than the one given. Use the keyboard below for help. (5 points)

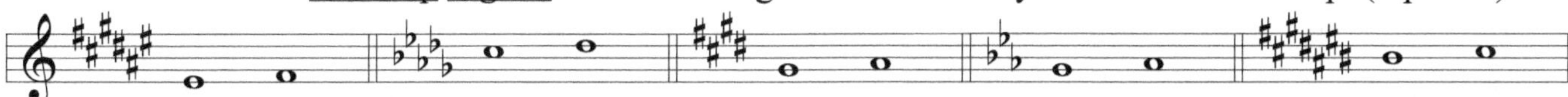

16. Draw the note a <u>whole step</u> **<u>lower</u>** than the one given. Use the keyboard below for help. (5 points)

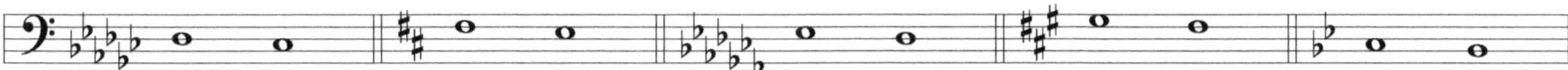

17. Each of these chords should have a Do (1), Mi (3), & Sol (5).
Fill in the missing note for each chord in both clefs to create a root position triad. (8 points)

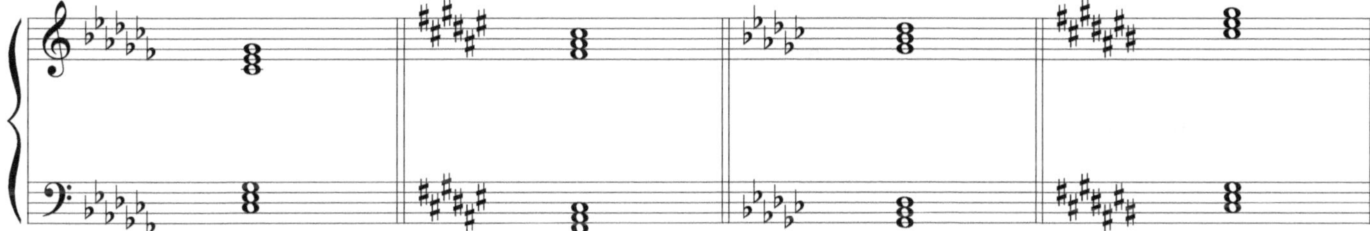

18. Draw a whole note above the given note to create the requested harmonic intervals. (8 points)

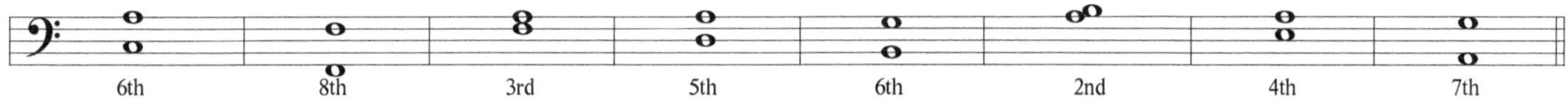

19. Write the note names and solfege directly under each note in the following examples. Don't forget to add ♯/♭ if needed. (8 points- 1 point per correct measure: both solfege and notes must be correct)

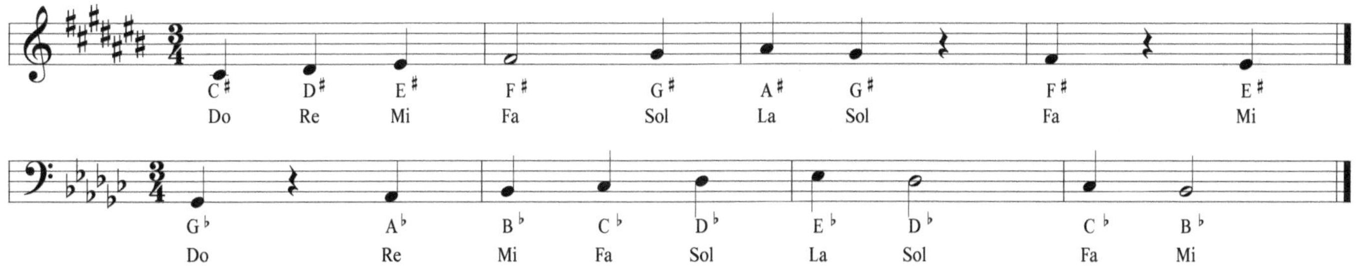

20. Check the English word that contains the same sound as the given IPA symbol. (8 points)

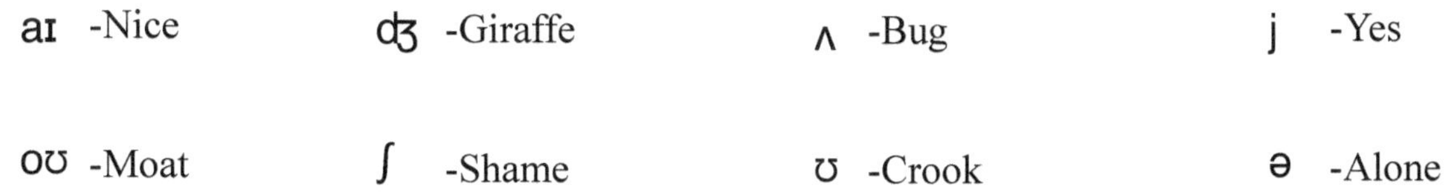

21. For the following questions, check the correct choice that best describes how the Italian/Latin word would be pronounced. The IPA spelling is provided for you, in parentheses, after the word. (4 points)

grazia (grat:tsja) - graht-see-a

chi (ki) - key

terzetto (tertset:to) - tare-tset-toh

deciso (detʃizo) - date-cheese-oh

22. Fill in the correct answer using the musical terms in this level. (5 points)

a. An_____opera_____is a play in which the characters sing rather than speak, accompanied by instruments.

b. _____più mosso_____means "more lively, faster."

c. A_____whole step_____is the interval of a Major 2nd; consists of 2 half steps, e.g. Do-Re

d. A_____diphthong_____is a vowel with two sounds.

e. _____andantino_____is a little faster tempo than *andante.*

23. For the following questions about Mozart & Mendelssohn, write the correct word or composer in the space provided. (5 points)

a. _____Mozart_____was buried in a common grave.

b. Mendelssohn was ___38___ years old when he died.

c. Mozart toured Europe with his sister _____Nannerl_____.

d. Mozart was friends with the composer Franz Joseph _____Haydn_____.

e. Mendelssohn wrote the famous Christmas carol _____Hark! The Herald Angels Sing_____.

REFERENCES

Grout, Donald. *A History of Western Music.* New York, NY: W.W. Norton & Company, Inc., 1996.

Moriarty, John. *Diction*. Boston, MA: E. C. Schirmer Music Company, 1975.

Music Teachers' Association of California. *Certificate of Merit Voice Syllabus.* San Francisco: Music Teachers' Association of California, 2011.

Piston, Walter. *Harmony, Fifth Edition.* New York, NY: W.W. Norton & Company, Inc., 1987.

Plantinga, Leon. *Romantic Music, A History of Musical Style in Nineteenth-Century Europe.* New York, NY: W.W. Norton & Company, Inc., 1984.

Randel, Don Michael. *The Harvard Biographical Dictionary of Music.* Cambridge, Massachusetts: The Belknap Press of Harvard University Press, 1996.

Randel, Don Michael. *Harvard Concise Dictionary of Music.* Cambridge, Massachusetts: The Belknap Press of Harvard University Press, 1978.

Rushton, Julian. *Classical Music, A Concise History from Gluck to Beethoven.* London, England: Thames and Hudson Ltd., 1986.

The New Grove Dictionary of Music and Musicians. http://www.oxfordmusiconline.com., 2011

www.ingramcontent.com/pod-product-compliance
Lightning Source LLC
LaVergne TN
LVHW061256100826
845148LV00008B/1148
* 9 7 8 1 5 2 4 9 1 4 3 9 4 *